UNSWEETENED HISTORY

VOLUME I

AADITYA JAISWAL

Made with ❤ on the Notion Press Platform
www.notionpress.com

This book is dedicated to millions of Hindus who suffered
under the tyrannical rule of invaders, and to the diabolical
historians, who tried to hide the truth.

Contents

Contents

Foreword

For too long, the history of India has been presented through a lens that obscures more than it reveals. A carefully constructed narrative, often driven by political expediency, ideological biases, a desire to avoid uncomfortable truths, the subtle influence of cultural hegemony, or even the unintentional perpetuation of outdated scholarship, has resulted in a distorted picture of our past. This book seeks to rectify that imbalance, to peel back the layers of misrepresentation, and to present a more complete and honest account of India's complex and often turbulent journey. It is an attempt to excavate the buried truths, to illuminate the shadows cast by selective amnesia, and to offer a more authentic portrayal of the multifaceted forces that have shaped the Indian subcontinent, acknowledging the intricate and ever-evolving tapestry of its historical experiences, and recognizing the inherent subjectivity of historical interpretation, while striving for objectivity through rigorous methodology.

This book is a quest to restore the voices that have been silenced, to acknowledge the suffering that has been ignored, and to confront the uncomfortable aspects of our shared heritage with courage, intellectual honesty, and a commitment to rigorous scholarship. It is an exploration of the intricate interplay of social, economic, political, and cultural forces that have shaped India's destiny, recognizing the agency of all actors involved, from the powerful rulers to the ordinary people whose lives were impacted by historical events, and acknowledging the complex and often unintended consequences of historical actions, as well as the lasting impact of those actions on subsequent generations, and the ways in which historical memory is used to justify present-day actions.

We must move beyond the simplistic narratives of heroes and villains, the sanitized accounts of linear progress, and the romanticized versions of our past that often serve to reinforce existing power structures, perpetuate harmful stereotypes, and obscure the complex realities of historical processes. We must delve into the messy reality of human experience, acknowledging the contradictions, the ambiguities, and the moral complexities that characterize historical events. This is a history of power and its abuse, of faith and its manipulation, of cultural exchange and its violent clashes, and of the enduring human spirit in the face of adversity. It is a history that has been selectively edited, deliberately misinterpreted, and often outright fabricated, not to replace one biased account with another, but to strive for a more balanced, nuanced, and evidence-based understanding. It is a call for a critical engagement with historical sources, urging readers to question the motivations behind the narratives they encounter, to be aware of the inherent biases in historical records, to examine the context in which those records were created, to consider the limitations of available evidence, and to seek out diverse perspectives from a wide range of primary and secondary sources, recognizing that historical truth is often a matter of interpretation and debate, and that the process of historical inquiry is itself a historical phenomenon, shaped by the social and political context in which it takes place.

The reader will encounter accounts that may challenge

their preconceived notions, forcing them to reconsider long-held beliefs and to question the narratives they have been taught, often from an early age, through formal education and informal cultural transmission. They will find evidence that contradicts the sanitized versions of history that have been widely disseminated through textbooks, popular culture, and even academic circles, leading them to examine the processes by which historical narratives are constructed and maintained, and to understand the role of power in shaping historical memory, and the ways in which historical narratives are used to construct and reinforce social and political identities, and to justify social and political actions. They will be confronted with the undeniable fact that the past is not always a pleasant story, and that ignoring the darker chapters does a disservice to the present, hindering our ability to learn from past mistakes, to address present-day inequalities, and to build a more just and equitable future. This book encourages a deeper examination of the sources, a critical analysis of the methodologies used by historians, and a willingness to challenge established interpretations, fostering a spirit of intellectual curiosity, a commitment to lifelong learning, and a recognition that historical understanding is an ongoing and evolving process, subject to revision as new evidence emerges and new perspectives are brought to bear, and that the ethical implications of historical interpretation are profound.

This book is not about rewriting history to fit a particular agenda, but about reclaiming the right to interpret our own past, to engage in a robust and open dialogue about the forces that have shaped our nation, and to participate in the ongoing process of historical understanding. It is about restoring balance, acknowledging the full spectrum of our heritage, and fostering a deeper understanding of the forces that have shaped India. It is an invitation to engage with the past critically, to question received wisdom, to examine primary sources with fresh eyes, to consider the social and political context in which historical events unfolded, to acknowledge the impact of power dynamics, to recognize the role of individual agency and collective action, and to embrace the complexities of our shared legacy, even when those complexities are painful or unsettling. Only by confronting the entirety of our past, the triumphs and the tragedies, the moments of glory and the periods of shame, can we truly illuminate the path to a more truthful, reconciled, and ultimately stronger future. It is a journey that requires courage, intellectual humility, and a willingness to challenge our own assumptions, but it is a journey that is essential for the health and well-being of our nation, a journey that demands we become active participants in the construction of our own historical understanding, and a journey that recognizes the ongoing and evolving nature of historical interpretation. Both author and reader have a responsibility to approach the past with a critical and open mind, to engage with diverse perspectives, to consider the ethical implications of historical narratives, and to contribute to a more nuanced and inclusive understanding of our shared history. Moreover, it is a journey that must be undertaken with ethical responsibility, acknowledging the potential for historical narratives to be used for both constructive and destructive purposes, and striving to create a history that promotes understanding, reconciliation, and justice. The process of historical inquiry is not merely an intellectual exercise, but a moral imperative, a continuous effort to understand ourselves, our communities, and our place in the world, and to use that understanding to build a better future. The reader is not a passive recipient of information, but an active participant in the construction of historical knowledge, and must approach the material presented with a critical and discerning eye.

Preface

"Unsweetened History" is not a mere chronicle of events; it is an excavation of the soul of India, a defiant act against the systematic erasure of our collective memory. It is a direct challenge to the comfortable narratives that have been spoon-fed to generations, narratives that have intentionally obscured the harsh realities of our past. This book is a declaration of independence from the intellectual shackles of a carefully constructed historical consensus, a consensus that has, for far too long, prioritized political expediency over historical accuracy.

This is not a romanticized retelling, a saccharine ode to the conquerors and invaders who sought to subjugate our land. Instead, it is a surgical dissection, a meticulous examination of the wounds inflicted upon our nation, a resolute effort to tear down the veils of deception that have shrouded our history since our earliest encounters with formalized education. It is an act of intellectual rebellion, a refusal to accept the distorted images of our past that have been used to pacify, to manipulate, and ultimately, to erode the very foundations of the Hindu identity.

"Unsweetened History" unfolds as a series of meticulously researched chapters, each dedicated to a specific, often overlooked, incident from our past. These incidents, whether deliberately airbrushed, inadequately disseminated, or ruthlessly suppressed, represent crucial turning points in India's narrative—pivotal moments that have been deliberately excised or distorted to fit a prefabricated narrative. This book is a determined initiative to illuminate these neglected or misrepresented chapters, to reveal the raw, unvarnished truth about the unwavering Hindu resistance against the brutal tyranny of despotic Muslim monarchs.

The calculated suppression of such heinous acts is nothing short of historical treachery. I vehemently denounce the historians who have chosen to prioritize ideological conformity over the pursuit of truth, who have sacrificed the integrity of historical scholarship on the altar of political appeasement. This book is a direct confrontation with their legacy—a demand for accountability, a call for intellectual restitution.

Beyond the mere exposure of these concealed truths, "Unsweetened History" is a fervent attempt to reignite a sense of pride, a spirit of resilience, and a profound understanding of our heritage among Hindus. For too long, our culture, our traditions, and our very identity have been under relentless assault by those who seek to undermine our collective memory, often by selectively highlighting the alleged treachery of a handful of individuals. While it is undeniable that some rulers succumbed to the pressures of the time, betraying their faith and aligning themselves with their oppressors, these instances are anomalies, not the norm. To allow the actions of a few to overshadow the countless acts of valor, the unwavering dedication, and the enduring sacrifices of our true heroes would be a profound travesty.

Innumerable "shoorveers" (warriors), whose names have been unjustly relegated to the footnotes of history, dedicated their lives to safeguarding the sanctity of Indian culture and religion. Their contributions, often deliberately marginalized or minimized, were instrumental in preserving the very essence of our civilization. Consider, for example, the indomitable spirit of Chhatrapati Shivaji Maharaj, whose unwavering commitment to "swaraj" (self-rule) stands as a beacon of resistance, a testament to the enduring power of the Hindu spirit. His was not a lone struggle, but a culmination of countless acts of defiance, a symphony of resistance against overwhelming odds.

It is my deepest aspiration that this book will serve as a transformative force, shattering the meticulously constructed edifice of falsehoods that have been erected around these heroes by our "secular" historians. I yearn to ignite a renewed appreciation for our rich and complex past, a deeper understanding of the challenges we face in the present, and a stronger foundation for the generations to come. This is not merely a book; it is a declaration of intellectual independence, a reclamation of our stolen heritage, a restoration of our rightful pride, and a resounding call to remember, to honor, and to reclaim our true history.

Prologue

The Echoes of Silence

The dust of ages settles thick upon the pages of history, obscuring the vibrant hues of truth beneath a pallid veneer of accepted narrative. Within these shadowed depths, the whispers of forgotten battles and silenced voices linger, a testament to the systematic erasure of India's soul. For too long, we have been fed a diet of sweetened fables, palatable to the palate of political expediency, but devoid of the raw, unadulterated essence of our past.

This is not a tale spun from the threads of romanticized heroism, nor a lament for lost empires. It is a journey into the heart of a wound that has festered for centuries, a wound inflicted by the relentless march of invaders who sought not merely to conquer, but to obliterate the very spirit of Hindustan. The echoes of their brutality reverberate through the corridors of time, a constant reminder of the price paid for our survival. Yet, these echoes have been muted, deliberately muffled by the custodians of a carefully curated history.

We have been taught to celebrate the architects of our subjugation, to venerate the hands that wielded the sword of oppression. The true heroes, the defenders of Dharma, the custodians of our cultural heritage, have been relegated to the footnotes, their sacrifices dismissed, their valor diminished. Their stories, like embers buried beneath ash, have been left to smolder, threatening to extinguish altogether.

This book is a defiant act of excavation, a relentless pursuit of the buried embers, a desperate attempt to fan them into a roaring flame. It is a rebellion against the intellectual tyranny that has dictated our understanding of the past, a refusal to accept the distorted images that have been used to pacify and control. "Unsweetened History" is a scalpel, wielded with precision and purpose, to dissect the layers of deception and expose the raw nerve of truth.

We will delve into the forgotten chapters, the incidents deliberately airbrushed from the grand narrative, the moments of resistance that have been systematically suppressed. We will confront the uncomfortable truths, the brutal realities of despotic rule, and the unwavering resilience of the Hindu spirit. We will shine a light on the "shoorveers," the countless warriors whose names have been unjustly consigned to oblivion, the guardians of our culture who stood against overwhelming odds.

This is not merely an academic exercise. It is a reclamation of our stolen heritage, a restoration of our rightful pride, a call to remember, to honor, and to reclaim our true history. For within these unsweetened truths lies the strength to confront the challenges of the present and forge a future rooted in the enduring legacy of our ancestors. The silence ends here. The echoes will be heard.

Acknowledgements

"Unsweetened History" is a testament to the power of shared knowledge and unwavering support. This book is the culmination of a journey made possible by the inspiration and encouragement of many, and I am deeply grateful to each individual who has contributed.

My intellectual awakening began with the profound works of Mr. Sandeep Balakrishna. His unflinching commitment to historical accuracy and his ability to excavate the often-buried narratives of our past have been a beacon, guiding my own research. His books, in particular, have served as invaluable companions. The dynamic and engaging presentations of Ms. Keerthika Govindhaswamy on her "Keerthi History" YouTube channel provided crucial insights and ignited a deeper passion for historical truth. It was Medha D. Bhaskaran Ma'am, with her captivating narratives, who sparked my interest in the intricate tapestry of our history, opening my eyes to the stories that echo through time. Without these individuals, the seed of this book would never have taken root.

I am profoundly grateful to Mr. U.K. Jha, Principal of The Ekayanaa School, Indore. His unwavering belief in this project and his consistent encouragement provided the necessary confidence to persevere.

The initial spark of my writing journey was ignited by Mrs. Renu Kasliwal. Her encouragement to explore the power of words, to weave narratives that resonate, set me on the path that led to this book. I am forever thankful for her early guidance and her belief in my potential to tell these important stories.

To Dr. Madhvi Singh and Mrs. Aarti Pandey, I extend my heartfelt appreciation for their constant support and unwavering belief in my abilities. Their encouragement was a source of strength throughout the writing process, providing me with the motivation to keep going even when faced with the weight of historical complexities.

A special thank you to Akshat Gupta sir for his insightful feedback and consistent encouragement. His belief in the importance of this work, and his willingness to share his expertise, was a powerful motivator, particularly as I navigated the sensitive and often contested terrains of our history.

My closest friends, Aryan Jain, Kopal Kasliwal, Anusha G., and Palash J., deserve immense gratitude. Their unwavering support, understanding, and friendship provided a much-needed respite and encouragement during the long hours of research and writing. Their presence was a constant reminder that I was not alone in this endeavor, that the stories I was unearthing mattered to those around me.

To my sisters-in-spirit, Aanya S. Thakur and Siya K., I offer my sincere thanks for their unwavering support and the invaluable strength of sisterhood they provided. Their understanding and encouragement were a source of strength, reminding me of the importance of sharing these stories with future generations.

Words cannot express the depth of my gratitude to my parents. Their unwavering love, support, and sacrifices have been the foundation upon which I have built my life and my work. They instilled in me the values of perseverance, integrity, and a thirst for knowledge.

My beloved nani has been a constant source of encouragement and wisdom. Her unwavering belief in me, her stories of our heritage, and her constant blessings have been a tremendous source of strength, connecting me to the rich cultural tapestry of our past.

I would also like to express my sense of obligation to Adv. Shivani P. Jaiswal, who helped me during times of research and guided me through all the legal requirements.

Finally, I extend my heartfelt thanks to my extended family members and friends who have offered their support, encouragement, and understanding throughout this journey. Each of you has played a part in bringing this book to fruition. I am particularly grateful for the shared memories and stories that have enriched my understanding of our history.

"Unsweetened History" is a collective effort, a testament to the power of shared knowledge and unwavering support. It is my sincere hope that this book will contribute to a deeper understanding of our past, and inspire future generations to explore the rich tapestry of India's history with a renewed sense of pride, curiosity, and a commitment to truth.

CHAPTER ONE

Bahadur Shah Zafar: The Last Mughal 'Traitor'

The haunting echoes of a bygone era resonate through the poignant couplet, "Ghaziyoñ meñ bū rahegī jab tak imān kī, Takht London tak chalegī tegh Hindostān kī," which translates to the enduring scent of faith in the hearts of our Ghazis, ensuring that the sword of Hindustan will continue to gleam before the throne of London. This declaration, steeped in a fervent nationalism, seems to emerge from a place of profound delusion, particularly when one considers the historical context of its author, Bahadur Shah Zafar. This last Mughal emperor, who presided over the crumbling remnants of a once-mighty empire, found himself ensnared in a web of servility, vice, poetic aspirations, indulgence in wine, and a reckless lifestyle that ultimately led to his downfall.

Zafar's delusions were not merely personal fantasies; they were emblematic of a larger, tragic narrative. Syed Ahmad Khan, a prominent figure in the early movements for Pakistan, recounted one of Zafar's most bizarre beliefs: he fancied himself capable of transforming into a fly or gnat, a whimsical notion that he believed would allow him to traverse borders and glean knowledge of distant lands. This peculiar self-perception might be excused, given that his authority had dwindled to the confines of the Red Fort, where he was acutely aware of his own diminished stature. Living under the watchful eye of the East India Company, he relied on a meager monthly pension of one lakh rupees, a sum that came with the price of allowing British troops to occupy his palace. His existence was marked by a constant, gnawing fear that the moment he drew his last breath, the British would strip him of this meager allowance and the few privileges he clung to.

Moreover, Zafar was not just a prisoner of circumstance; he was also ensnared in the manipulative grasp of his favorite wife, Zeenat Mahal, who wielded considerable influence over him, further complicating his already precarious position.

The Wahabi Movement, often misconstrued as a struggle for independence, was, in reality, a declaration of war against what was perceived as infidel India. In this context, Zafar's role during the Great Revolt of 1857, often romanticized by historians as that of a tragic hero, reveals a more complex and troubling reality. While many in the secular narrative of Indian history paint him as a freedom fighter, the truth is that Zafar's actions during this tumultuous period were marked by betrayal and cowardice. William Dalrymple's portrayal of Zafar as a "tragic figure of the eponymous monarch... and abidingly fond of the arts of peace" is a testament to the perverse talent required to elevate such a weakling to the status of a hero.

Fully aware of his own pitiable condition, Zafar went to great lengths to demonstrate his loyalty to the British, ensuring that he was not perceived as a threat to their authority. This precarious balance was shattered on the morning of May 11, 1857, when a group of triumphant sepoys stormed the palace, having just killed British troops in Meerut. They clamored for Zafar to assume leadership of the Great Revolt, a request that left him utterly bewildered. In fact, he was largely unaware that the revolt had erupted so close to Delhi. The urgency of the situation became apparent to his courtiers and his personal physician, Hakim Ahsanullah Khan, who recognized that immediate action was necessary to prevent chaos.

Caught between the proverbial rock and a hard place, Zafar faced an impossible dilemma. Supporting the sepoys would undoubtedly provoke the wrath of the British, while failing to do so would jeopardize his own safety. The palpable fear that gripped the aged Mughal is vividly captured in the diary of his news writer, Munshi Jivanlal, who noted the complete cessation of trade in the city, as shops were emptied and a turbulent mob of soldiers demanded that the King accompany them through the streets, flanked by his army. Upon returning to the palace, Zafar was met with a scene that starkly illustrated his powerlessness: soldiers, once mere sepoys, now emboldened, had invaded the Diwan-i-Khas, hurling insults at him and even tugging at his luxurious white beard. In a state of panic, Zafar retreated to his private quarters, surrounded by servants, lamenting his misfortune and shedding tears over his dire predicament.

Ultimately, he capitulated to the demands of the sepoys, reluctantly accepting the title of "emperor of Hindustan" as they sought a figurehead to rally around. However, this title was bestowed upon him not out of respect, but rather out of desperation for leadership. Zafar's acceptance of this role was marked by betrayal, as he failed to provide the strong guidance the sepoys desperately needed. Acharya R.C. Majumdar's analysis underscores this point, noting that the sepoys were not solely to blame for the disarray; Zafar's advanced age, lack of administrative experience, and penchant for poetry left him ill-equipped to lead a rebellion.

Instead of rallying the sepoys with steely resolve, Zafar offered them pious platitudes, urging them to abandon worldly pursuits in favor of a life of Fakirs. British historians have noted that Zafar, despite being thrust into a position of leadership, would likely have preferred to shy away from such responsibilities had he been left to his own devices.

As the conflict escalated, Zafar maintained a façade of resistance while simultaneously opening a secret channel of communication with the British, offering them his support in quelling the sepoys. R.C. Majumdar's observations reveal that Zafar harbored no confidence in the sepoys or sympathy for their cause, and even after aligning himself with them, he remained loyal to the British. He sent letters to British military officers, including the Lieutenant Governor of Agra, detailing the movements and positions of the sepoys in Delhi. The testimony of Ahsanullah Khan during the trial following the revolt, along with Zafar's own admissions, further corroborate this treachery.

One of the most chilling acts of betrayal occurred a month into the Great Revolt. While sepoys fought valiantly in his name, Zafar sent a message to General T. Reed, the British commander besieging Delhi, offering to open the gates for British troops in exchange for guarantees of his life and pension. The Gomastha, Fateh Mohamed, conveyed Zafar's eagerness to negotiate terms with the British, revealing the depths of his desperation.

As the revolt continued, Zafar's family, including his wife Zeenat Mahal and various princes, began reaching out to the British, expressing their loyalty and willingness to assist them. The entries in British diaries from that time reflect a growing correspondence with Zafar's family, indicating a clear desire to align with the British against the sepoys.

The overwhelming evidence points to a stark conclusion: Bahadur Shah Zafar, far from leading the First War of Indian Independence, actively betrayed it. Majumdar's assertion that Zafar and his family betrayed not only the mutineers but the entire nation resonates with chilling clarity. The terms of Zafar's betrayal were alarmingly cheap, as he was willing to sell himself for a pittance, despite his grandiose claims of being an emperor.

Ultimately, the British crushed the Great Revolt before Zafar could fully execute his betrayal, leading to his abject surrender. The subsequent narrative of his exile to Burma, where he spent his final days in misery and squalor, serves as a tragic epilogue to a life marked by delusion and betrayal.

In a disheartening twist of fate, the legacy of Bahadur Shah Zafar was further tarnished by the visit of former Prime Minister Manmohan Singh to his grave in Yangon in 2012, where he offered a Fateha (prayer) to the man who had betrayed his people. This act underscores the need for India to confront and recover from the complex and often painful truths of its history.

CHAPTER TWO

The Twilight of Hindu Bengal: The Tragic Saga of Raja Sitaram Ray

The legend of Raja Sitaram Ray, even decades after his fall, echoed through Bengal's villages and fields, a testament to his enduring place in the region's heart. Bankim Chandra Chattopadhyaya, Bengal's literary giant, enshrined him in his novel "Sitaram," crafting a hero who resonated with the soul of a people. Jadunath Sarkar, the respected historian, confirmed the novel's power, recognizing how it imbued Sitaram with a romantic aura, ensuring his memory would live on as long as Bengali was spoken. Yet, "Sitaram" was more than fiction; it was a mirror reflecting the harsh realities faced by Bengali Hindus under Murshid Quli Khan's rule and the broader Mughal dominance. The lack of an English translation, a lamentable gap, has kept this vital chapter of Bengal's history from reaching a wider audience.

Our focus, however, is not just on the fictional hero, but on the historical Sitaram Das, a man who rose from humble Kayastha roots to become the last significant independent Hindu ruler in Bengal. His life, a story of meteoric rise and tragic decline, mirrors the larger struggle of Hindu resistance against the expanding Mughal Empire, a narrative often pushed to the margins of historical record.

Sitaram Das was born in a year of political turmoil, the same year Aurangzeb seized the Mughal throne. Yet, his early life was relatively peaceful. His grandfather, Hima Das, served as a revenue official under Shuja, the Subahdar of Bengal. His father, Udaynarayan, was a Tehsildar under the Faujdar of Bhushna. In 1664, Udaynarayan's skills caught the eye of Shaista Khan, the new governor of Bengal, who summoned him to Dacca.

Sitaram grew up in his maternal uncle's home in Katwa, demonstrating exceptional intelligence. He mastered Sanskrit, absorbing Bengal's rich literary and devotional heritage, and could recite Chandidas and Jayadeva from memory. Recognizing the importance of Persian for advancement, he also became proficient in the language. He further honed his martial skills, mastering horsemanship, swordsmanship, and other essential disciplines.

Shaista Khan, recognizing Sitaram's potential, recruited him into his service. Sitaram's first major opportunity came when he volunteered to quell the Pathan rebel Karim Khan, who was terrorizing the Satair Paragana. Shaista Khan placed him in charge of a small army. In a fierce battle, Sitaram defeated Karim Khan, earning Shaista Khan's admiration and the jagir of Naldi.

This marked the beginning of Sitaram's remarkable ascent.

Sitaram quickly built a strong army, demonstrating his exceptional military leadership. He appointed Ramrup Ghosh, known as "Mena Hati," a renowned wrestler and soldier, as his commander-in-chief. Mena Hati, famed for killing a small elephant with his bare hands, became a symbol of strength and loyalty.

With his army in place, Sitaram focused on restoring order in the Naldi region, suppressing Afghan banditry and establishing peace. His efforts were successful, and he was hailed as a savior by the people, likened to the Grama Devata, Nishanath.

By 1684, Sitaram had established a small kingdom, expanding his territory by acquiring talukas from neighboring Paraganas. He attracted a diverse following, including adventurers, former dacoits, mercenaries, and merchants, drawn to his reputation as a generous leader.

The Mughal Subahdars, preoccupied with the political turmoil in Delhi, did not interfere with Sitaram's growing power. Sitaram maintained cordial relations with Delhi and the Bengal Subahdars by making regular payments. He also served as a buffer against Afghan dacoits, a role appreciated by the authorities.

Around this time, Sitaram went on a pilgrimage to Gaya to perform the last rites of his parents. From Gaya, he traveled to Delhi, where he sought an audience with Aurangzeb's court. His request was granted, and he petitioned the emperor to make him a Mughal vassal. This move, while seemingly contradictory to his eventual independence, was a shrewd political maneuver, legitimizing his authority.

In 1688, Sitaram was bestowed with the title of Raja of Naldi and given charge of Southern Bengal up to the Sunderbans. Upon his return, a grand Rajyabhishekam was performed, and he became known as Raja Sitaram Ray.

However, Sitaram lacked a capital. He established a fortified city named Mohammadpur, built from scratch. Jadunath Sarkar described Mohammadpur as a fortified settlement with earthen embankments, a fosse, and natural barriers provided by marshes and the Madhumati River. Sitaram built temples, palaces, offices, storehouses, and dug tanks for fresh water. Mohammadpur quickly became a thriving commercial center.

Sitaram's newfound royalty fueled his ambitions. He expanded his army and arsenal, and through military campaigns, he subdued neighboring zamindars and chieftains, annexing their territories. By 1704, he had become a formidable power in the region.

However, his ambition ultimately led to his downfall. Around this time, Murshid Quli Khan was in conflict with Azim-us-Shan, the Subahdar of Bengal. Azim appointed his relative, Sayyid Abu Turab, as the Faujdar of Bhushna, with the intent of curbing Sitaram's power. Abu Turab, upon assuming his post, unleashed a reign of terror, targeting Hindu tax defaulters and forcibly converting them to Islam.

Sitaram, angered by Abu Turab's actions, retaliated by

halting payments to the Mughal treasury. Abu Turab, seeking to punish Sitaram, requested military assistance from Azim and Murshid Quli Khan. However, his requests were ignored due to the political turmoil in Delhi and the animosity between Azim and Murshid Quli Khan.

Frustrated, Abu Turab launched an attack on Sitaram in 1713. His forces were decisively defeated, and in the Battle of Barasia, Sitaram's army, led by Mena Hati, killed Abu Turab.

Murshid Quli Khan, now the Subahdar of Bengal, viewed Abu Turab's defeat as a personal affront. He considered Sitaram's killing of a Muslim Faujdar an act of defiance.

He appointed his brother-in-law, Baksh Ali Khan, as the new Faujdar of Bhushna and sent a strong force against Sitaram. He also ordered the zamindars in Sitaram's territories to assist Baksh Ali Khan.
Murshid Quli Khan's Hindu loyalists, Sangram Singh and Dayaram Rai, also joined the campaign against Sitaram. Sitaram, facing overwhelming odds, prepared to defend his kingdom. He had to defend two forts, Bhushna and Mohammadpur, simultaneously.

Murshid Quli Khan's forces, recognizing the difficulty of capturing Mohammadpur by direct assault, resorted to treachery. Dayaram Rai assassinated Mena Hati, a devastating blow to Sitaram's army. Mena Hati's severed head was paraded through Murshidabad.

Sitaram, upon learning of Mena Hati's death, evacuated the civilian population of Mohammadpur to Kolkata. He then prepared to face the final battle.

Baksh Ali Khan attacked the fort from the south, while Dayaram Rai attacked from the east. Sitaram's forces fought valiantly, but they were overwhelmed, and he was captured along with his family.

Dayaram Rai bound Sitaram in chains and escorted him to Murshidabad, where he was paraded through the streets. Dayaram Rai also seized a large portion of Sitaram's treasury and transported it to Natore. For his treachery, Murshid Quli Khan appointed Dayaram Rai as the Raja of Dighapatiya.

Murshid Quli Khan sentenced Sitaram Ray to death and imprisoned his family for life.

Jadunath Sarkar, who visited Mohammadpur in the 1940s, described the ruins of Sitaram's kingdom. His palaces had crumbled, his lakes were choked with mud and weeds, and his family had been scattered. Even the deities he worshipped had abandoned his temples.

The fall of Sitaram Ray marked the end of the last significant independent Hindu kingdom in Bengal, a tragic tale of ambition, betrayal, and the relentless advance of Mughal power. His story serves as a poignant reminder of the struggles faced by Hindu rulers in a changing political landscape, a landscape where loyalty was often a fragile commodity and power was ruthlessly pursued. The ruins of Mohammadpur, silent witnesses to a vanished era, stand as a testament to the enduring legacy of Raja Sitaram Ray, a symbol of resistance and a reminder of the fading light of Hindu sovereignty in Bengal.

CHAPTER THREE

FROM FILTH TO FINANCE: MURSHID QULI KHAN'S ABHORRENT REVENUE INNOVATION

Murshid Quli Khan's ascension to the governorship of Bengal marked a pivotal, and brutally transformative, chapter in the region's history. From his meticulously planned capital in Murshidabad, he crafted a system of revenue administration that, while undeniably efficient in extracting wealth, was built upon a foundation of terror and unyielding control. His legacy, as documented by both official chronicles and the stark realities faced by the populace, paints a picture of a ruler who prioritized absolute authority and financial gain above all else, leaving a trail of suffering in his wake.

Upon establishing Murshidabad as his center of power, Murshid Quli Khan embarked on a comprehensive restructuring of the Bengal Subah. He divided the region into thirteen distinct circles, or Chaklas, each acting as a major administrative unit. These Chaklas were further subdivided into thirteen smaller tracts, known as Jahgirs, each placed under the control of a Jahgirdar or Zamindar. These individuals were held personally accountable to Quli, ensuring a direct line of control and a clear chain of responsibility.

Beyond the Jahgirs, Quli established twenty-five Khalsas, directly managed lands within the Chaklas. These Khalsas were farmed out to revenue contractors, a system designed to maximize revenue collection by shifting the burden of extraction to private individuals. This layered system of control, with its intricate web of accountability, allowed Quli to exert a firm grip on the financial resources of Bengal.

Furthermore, the establishment of his own mint in Murshidabad served as an undeniable symbol of his growing autonomy. Minting coinage was a prerogative traditionally reserved for sovereign rulers, and Quli's move signaled his increasing independence from the Mughal court. This act, coupled with his administrative reforms, solidified his position as the de facto ruler of Bengal.

The effectiveness of Quli's revenue system was widely acknowledged, even by contemporary chroniclers. Ghulam

Husain Salim Zaidpuri, in his "Riyaz-us-Salatin," provides a detailed account of the system's operation. According to Zaidpuri, Quli's Amils (revenue collectors) deployed Shiqdars and Amins to every village, conducting meticulous surveys of cultivated and waste lands. These lands were then leased back to tenants on a plot-by-plot basis, with agricultural loans (Taqavi) provided to poorer farmers to encourage cultivation. Quli's focus on increasing both revenue and cultivated land area was evident in his comprehensive revenue roll, which documented rents in kind, land revenue, sair taxes (octroi), and fees from agricultural lands.

Quli's administration was also characterized by a focus on fiscal responsibility. He implemented stringent measures to reduce public expenditure, allowing him to remit significantly increased revenue to the Imperial Treasury. This combination of efficient revenue collection and cost-cutting measures contributed to the substantial wealth that flowed from Bengal to Delhi.

However, the apparent efficiency of Quli's revenue system masked a dark reality. His reforms were enforced through a regime of terror, where torture and ruthlessness were the primary tools of governance. While the system may have reduced the exploitation by multiple layers of intermediaries, it replaced them with a single, far more oppressive force. The cultivators, once squeezed by "double sets of leeches," now found themselves trapped in the "inescapable stranglehold of a giant boa constrictor," as aptly described.

Quli's methods were reminiscent of the brutal tactics employed by Balban, a 13th-century ruler known for his iron-fisted rule. Like Balban, Quli ruled according to Islamic law, maintaining a rigid social hierarchy and a chasmic distance between himself and his officials. Jahgirdars and Zamindars were denied direct access to him, with only Amils and Mutsadis allowed to submit petitions. Even then, approaching Quli was a terrifying ordeal, with officials quailing in his presence, "remaining standing breathless like statues."

He also enforced strict social protocols. Hindu Zamindars were prohibited from traveling in Palkis, even if it suited their status, and Amils and Mutsadis were forbidden from riding on horseback. Mansabdars were required to wear uniforms in his presence, further emphasizing his absolute authority.

Quli's paranoia and desire for complete control extended to his officialdom. He deliberately reduced his officials to a state of fear, ensuring that no one could challenge his authority. He believed that confident delegation of authority was a sign of weakness, a trait he despised.

The most chilling aspect of Quli's reign was the manner in which he enforced revenue collection. His methods surpassed even the most ruthless loan-sharking techniques of today. At the end of each month, Quli summoned his officials to the Diwan-Khana of his Chihel Satun palace, a hall of forty pillars. These officials were held in a state of quasi-imprisonment, subjected to the intimidating presence of his soldiers.

Quli meticulously examined their contracts and account books, searching for any discrepancies or outstanding dues. Officials who failed to meet their revenue targets were subjected to horrific torture. They were deprived of basic bodily functions, denied food and water, and prevented from answering calls of nature. This ordeal could last for weeks, with no amount of pleading for mercy swaying Quli's resolve.

The punishments inflicted were designed to break the spirit of the officials. They were suspended by their heels, their heads facing down, while sharp stones were rubbed on the soles of their feet. They were then beaten with iron rods and bamboo sticks, and flogged with cat o' nines until they lost consciousness. The flogging would resume once they regained their senses.

These savage punishments were the brainchild of Quli's peon, Nazir Ahmad, highlighting the extent to which brutality permeated his administration. The goal was simple: to extract the maximum amount of revenue, regardless of the human cost.

Even in cases where officials had genuinely exhausted all options, Quli's wrath was unrelenting. Hindu officials faced particularly harsh treatment. After enduring the standard torture, they were forced to prove their honesty. If Quli was convinced, he forcibly converted them and their families to Islam, adding religious persecution to his arsenal of oppression.

Perhaps the most revolting punishment was devised by Syed Razi Khan, Quli's son-in-law and Deputy Diwan. This "noxious pervert," as he is described, ordered the construction of a pit filled with human excrement, derisively named "Vaikunth," a sacred Hindu term.

Zamindars and Amils who had defaulted on their dues or

failed to meet their targets were subjected to this horrific punishment. They were tortured and then suspended by their feet, lowered into the pit until they were neck-deep in filth. They were then lifted and lowered repeatedly, until they agreed to pay their dues.

This level of cruelty, inflicted upon ranking officials, had a ripple effect throughout Bengal. The officials, in turn, subjected the populace to similar forms of oppression, creating a climate of fear and despair. The farmers of Bengal lived on the brink of impoverishment, their surplus wealth flowing directly into Quli's coffers.

Quli's relentless pursuit of revenue enabled him to remit vast sums of wealth to the Mughal treasury in Delhi. Each year, he sent one crore and three lakh rupees, both in cash and kind. The "Riyaz-us-Salatin" provides a vivid description of these remittances, detailing the caravans of wagons laden with treasure, escorted by hundreds of cavalry and infantry.

In addition to the revenue, Quli sent gifts of elephants, horses, buffaloes, deers, and other rarities, including European manufactures and presents received from Christians. These lavish gifts served to solidify his position with the Mughal court, while simultaneously draining Bengal of its resources.

Murshid Quli Khan's heartless exploitation of Bengal surpassed even the excesses of Shah Jahan, who had diverted the region's wealth to fund his extravagant projects. Quli's reign was a testament to the destructive power of unchecked ambition, where the pursuit of wealth and power was achieved at the cost of human suffering and the erosion of cultural identity. His legacy serves as a stark reminder of the importance of ethical governance and the dangers of unchecked authority.

CHAPTER FOUR

THE MONSTER OF GANDIKOTA

In the grand tapestry of Indian history, few figures evoke as much disdain as Mir Jumla, whose exploits during the Battle of Gandikota epitomize the treachery and cunning that characterized his rise to power. As a general under Sultan Qutub Shah of the Golconda Sultanate, Mir Jumla was not merely a military leader; he was a master of deceit, willing to sacrifice honor and integrity for the sake of ambition. His actions during this pivotal conflict reveal a man driven by a ruthless desire for dominance, willing to betray allies and exploit the vulnerabilities of his enemies.

The stage for the Battle of Gandikota was set against a backdrop of shifting allegiances and the relentless expansion of the Golconda Sultanate. The fort of Gandikota, a bastion of the Pemmasani Nayakas, stood as a significant obstacle to Mir Jumla's ambitions. Pemmasani Thimma Nayudu, the valiant commander of the fort, was known for his unwavering loyalty and fierce defense of his territory. The fort, with its imposing walls and strategic location, symbolized resistance against the encroaching Muslim powers. Yet, Mir Jumla, with his insatiable thirst for power, saw only an opportunity to exploit.

The battle commenced with a thunderous roar as Pemmasani Thimma Nayudu unleashed the might of his artillery. The Ramabanam, a massive cannon stationed at the fort's gate, fired a devastating shot that decimated a significant portion of Mir Jumla's forces, claiming the lives of three thousand men in an instant. This catastrophic loss sent shockwaves through Mir Jumla's ranks, forcing him to reevaluate his strategy. Rather than retreating in shame, he cunningly withdrew to Goriganuru, a strategic distance of twenty kilometers southeast of Gandikota, where he plotted his next move.

In the face of overwhelming firepower, Mir Jumla's mind, sharp and calculating, turned to treachery as a means to achieve his goals. In a move that would define his character, he reached out to the French gunners serving under Pemmasani Thimma Nayudu. The allure of additional wages proved irresistible, and the French gunners, swayed by the promise of wealth, revealed the vulnerable points along the Gandikota scarp where Mir Jumla's cannons could be transported. This act of betrayal was not merely a tactical maneuver; it was a reflection of Mir Jumla's willingness to exploit the weaknesses of his adversaries, showcasing his utter lack of scruples.

With the intelligence gained from the French gunners, Mir Jumla swiftly mobilized his forces, positioning four cannons to unleash a relentless barrage upon the fort. The sound of cannon fire echoed through the valleys, heralding the chaos that was to follow. The bombardment that ensued was unprecedented in its intensity. The Gandikota Kaifiyat, a historical account of the events, vividly describes the terror that gripped the inhabitants of the fort. The relentless cannonade was so overwhelming that it induced miscarriages among pregnant women and caused many men to succumb to shock. Yet, even this onslaught failed to dislodge Pemmasani Thimma Nayudu from his stronghold.

In a desperate bid to negotiate, Mir Jumla extended an offer to Nayudu—a proposition that seemed enticing. He proposed an exchange: the fort of Gandikota in return for the prized stronghold of Gutti and its surrounding dominions. While the offer appeared advantageous, Nayudu, wary of the treacherous nature of the Turushka, countered with his own terms. He demanded the immediate transfer of Gutti, along with the assurance of a garrison, before he would relinquish Gandikota. Mir Jumla, recognizing the precariousness of his position, declined Nayudu's terms but countered with a promise: vacate Gandikota, and he would grant Gutti without delay. Thimma Nayudu, after consulting with his ministers and advisors, deemed this an exceptional offer and, against his better judgment, agreed to the terms.

In the initial phase of his withdrawal, Nayudu sent away the Vigrahas, the sacred idols, along with their ornaments, to a secure location known as Raju Cheruvu. However, the enormity of the task at hand rendered it impossible to clear the fort entirely of its treasures—jewelry, artifacts, and the revered Murtis of Devatas, the wealth of generations. Thus, Nayudu made the heart-wrenching decision to bury these sacred relics within the ramparts of the fort, hoping to preserve them for posterity. As the final act of evacuation unfolded, Pemmasani Thimma Nayudu led his retinue, accompanied by the women of his harem and his loyal soldiers, from the fort. They camped in the town below, awaiting Mir Jumla's Parwana, the official decree granting them the fort of Gutti.

However, in a cruel twist of fate, Mir Jumla revealed his true nature. A cunning and ruthless plunderer, he had no intention of honoring his word. Instead of granting Nayudu the fort of Gutti, he issued a Parwana that designated the insignificant Hanuma Gutti, a mere shadow of the stronghold Nayudu had relinquished, as the reward for his trust. Cornered and humiliated, Pemmasani Thimma Nayudu had no choice but to accept this ignoble exchange, cursing Mir Jumla as he departed for Hanuma Gutti, where he would spend the remainder of his days in obscurity.

With the fort of Gandikota now firmly in his grasp, Mir Jumla unleashed a wave of destruction that would forever stain the pages of history. In a frenzy of Islamic zealotry, his troops slaughtered countless cows within the sacred precincts of the Madhavaswami Temple, desecrated the Murtis, and razed smaller temples to the ground, repurposing their remnants to construct the Jumma Masjid, a testament to their conquest. The Agraharas, the homes of Brahmin families, were confiscated, and the inhabitants expelled, marking a dark chapter in the region's history.

Mir Jumla proclaimed himself the Nawab of Gandikota and embarked on an ambitious campaign to fortify his newfound stronghold. He envisioned a grand transformation, erecting twenty-four bastions, imposing gates, opulent Mahals, and recreational parks. Among his many projects was the construction of a grand fountain, a symbol of his ambition, though it would remain devoid of water—a poignant metaphor for the hollow victories of his reign. In a bid to further enhance the fort's defenses, Mir Jumla commissioned the creation of two colossal cannons—a 48-Pounder and a 24-Pounder. To realize this vision, he enlisted the expertise of a French gunner and gunfounder named Claude Maille. Under Maille's guidance, the ambitious project commenced, requiring vast quantities of metal to cast the cannons. Tavernier, an eyewitness to this endeavor, noted that Maille was "supplied with copper for this purpose from all quarters." Yet, as the project progressed, the demand for metal outstripped supply, prompting Mir Jumla to resort to a shocking innovation—he ordered the collection of Hindu Murtis made of metal from temples across the region.

The temples that had once stood as bastions of faith and culture were raided, their metallic Vigrahas carted off to the fort, melted down in a frenzy of destruction. All but six Murtis, three seated on their heels and three towering ten feet high, were spared from this sacrilege. These sacred idols, drawn from the Madhavaswami Temple, resisted the flames, refusing to yield to the molten fate that befell their brethren. In a fit of rage and frustration, Mir Jumla summoned the Archakas, accusing them of bewitching the idols, a reflection of his desperation and the futility of his ambitions. Ultimately, Maille's efforts to forge the cannons met with failure, and he resigned from Mir Jumla's service, leaving Gandikota in disgrace. The perfidious conquest of Gandikota, however, was celebrated by the Golconda Sultanate as a crowning achievement for Mir Jumla. Sultan Qutub Shah honored him with the Nauroz-i-Khillat, a ceremonial bestowal of royal robes and gifts, a hollow recognition of his treachery.

In the aftermath of this tumultuous episode, Mir Jumla departed from Gandikota in 1652-53, seeking permission from the Sultan to embark on the Hajj pilgrimage, a journey that would take him far from the blood-soaked grounds of his conquest. Yet, a footnote remains in this tragic narrative—a reflection on the last descendant of the Vijayanagara Aravidu dynasty, Sri Ranga III, who coexisted with both Pemmasani Thimma Nayudu and Mir Jumla. Despite his strategic alliances and victories against various Muslim powers, the mystery lingers as to why he did not endeavor to reclaim Gandikota after Mir Jumla's departure.

The Battle of Gandikota, while an epic confrontation, serves as but a single page in the broader tapestry of history, a narrative woven with threads of Muslim treachery and the blind trust of Hindu leaders. The naivety of Pemmasani Thimma Nayudu, who placed his faith in Mir Jumla's word, stands as a cautionary tale—a reminder of the perils of misplaced trust in a world rife with duplicity. In the grand tapestry of history, the Battle of Gandikota remains a poignant reminder of the complexities of power, loyalty, and the inexorable march of fate. It is a tale that transcends time, echoing through the corridors of history, urging us to reflect on the lessons of the past as we navigate the challenges of the present and future. Mir Jumla, a figure of ambition and treachery, serves as a reminder of the darker aspects of human nature, where the pursuit of power can lead to betrayal and destruction. His legacy, marked by cunning and ruthlessness, continues to resonate, urging us to remain vigilant against the forces of deceit that can shape the course of history.

CHAPTER FIVE

NAROTTAM

In 17th-century Muscat, Hindu merchant Narottam's trade with the Portuguese soured with Commandant Pareira's arrival. Pareira's arrogance and greed sparked Narottam's quiet rebellion. He fueled local discontent and allied with the Yaruba Arabs, turning a trade dispute into a history-altering conflict.

Thatta, a bustling port city nestled along the banks of the Indus River, was a jewel in the crown of the Arghun dynasty in 1555. Its strategic location made it a crucial hub for trade between India, Central Asia, and the Persian Gulf. The city's wealth, derived from its thriving commerce, attracted merchants from far and wide, contributing to its cosmopolitan character. However, beneath the veneer of prosperity, simmering tensions threatened to disrupt the city's tranquility. Mirza Isa Khan I, a Tarkhan warlord, harbored ambitions to break free from the Arghun yoke. He saw an opportunity in the political instability plaguing Shah Hussain Arghun's reign. Isa Khan, known for his cunning and military prowess, sought to leverage the might of the

Portuguese, a formidable maritime power in the region.

The Portuguese, eager to expand their sphere of influence and secure lucrative trade routes, saw Isa Khan's request as a chance to gain a foothold in Thatta. A fleet, laden with soldiers and cannons, set sail for the Indus delta. However, by the time they arrived, Isa Khan had already achieved his objective. Shah Hussain Arghun, weakened by internal strife, had been decisively defeated. Isa Khan, now the master of Thatta, found himself in a precarious position. He had no intention of honoring his agreement with the Portuguese, fearing that they would become a greater threat than the Arghuns. The Portuguese, incensed by this betrayal, demanded their due. When Isa Khan refused, they unleashed a torrent of violence upon the city.

The sacking of Thatta was a brutal affair. The Portuguese soldiers, driven by greed and a thirst for revenge, plundered the city's opulent treasury, seizing vast quantities of gold and precious artifacts. They spared no one, indiscriminately slaughtering men, women, and children. The once-vibrant city was transformed into a scene of carnage and despair. The consequences of this pillage were far-reaching. The city's reputation as a safe haven for trade was tarnished, and its economy suffered a severe blow. The incident also exposed the vulnerability of Thatta to external forces, setting the stage for decades of instability and conflict. The memory of the Portuguese rampage lingered, casting a long shadow over the city's future.

The incident was not just a simple act of revenge, but a manifestation of the complex power dynamics of the 16th century. The Portuguese, driven by their imperial ambitions, sought to exploit the weaknesses of local rulers.

Their actions in Thatta demonstrated their willingness to use force to achieve their goals, regardless of the consequences. The fall of Thatta also highlights the challenges faced by regional powers in the face of European expansion. The Portuguese, with their superior naval technology and military organization, posed a formidable threat to the traditional power structures of the Indian Ocean world. This incident foreshadowed the growing influence of European powers in the region and the eventual decline of indigenous empires.

The chaos in Thatta continued until 1591 when the Mughal Emperor Akbar, known for his administrative acumen and military might, decided to bring the region under his control. He dispatched Abdul Rahim Khan-i-Khanan, a skilled general and statesman, to annex Thatta. The Mughal army, a well-disciplined force, swiftly subdued the local rulers, and Thatta became a part of the vast Mughal Empire. Akbar's annexation brought a period of relative stability to Thatta. The Mughals implemented a centralized administrative system, which helped to restore order and promote economic growth. The city once again became a vital center for trade, attracting merchants from across the empire. The Mughals also invested in infrastructure, building roads, bridges, and irrigation systems, which further boosted the region's prosperity.

However, Mughal rule was not without its challenges. The vastness of the empire and the diversity of its population created administrative complexities. Local rebellions and uprisings were not uncommon, and the Mughals had to constantly assert their authority. The city also experienced periods of famine and plague, which took a toll on its population. Despite these challenges, Thatta thrived under Mughal rule. The city's cultural life flourished, with poets, scholars, and artists patronized by the Mughal court. The city's architectural heritage also reflects the Mughal influence, with numerous mosques, tombs, and palaces built in the Mughal style.

The Mughal legacy in Thatta is a complex one. While the Mughals brought stability and prosperity, they also imposed their own cultural and administrative systems, which sometimes clashed with local traditions. The city's history under Mughal rule is a testament to the enduring influence of the Mughal Empire and its impact on the cultural and political landscape of South Asia. The relationship between the Sindhi Bhatia community and the Portuguese was marked by a complex mix of trade, cooperation, and conflict. The Bhatias, a mercantile community with a long history of seafaring and trade, played a crucial role in the economic life of the region. They were involved in trade with various parts of the Indian Ocean world, including the Portuguese settlements in India and the Persian Gulf.

Initially, the Bhatias and the Portuguese engaged in mutually beneficial trade. The Bhatias provided the Portuguese with access to local markets and goods, while the Portuguese offered protection and access to their vast trading network. However, as the Portuguese became more assertive in their control of trade, tensions began to rise. The incident involving Narottam's daughter and the Portuguese commandant Pareira in 1650 was a culmination of these simmering tensions. It exposed the cultural and religious differences that divided the two communities. The Portuguese, driven by their sense of superiority and their desire to impose their will, disregarded the Bhatias' cultural and religious sensitivities.

The incident also highlights the role of personal relationships in shaping historical events. Pareira's lust for Narottam's daughter and his disregard for her family's honor sparked a chain of events that ultimately led to the expulsion of the Portuguese from Muscat. The Bhatias' role in the expulsion of the Portuguese from Muscat demonstrates their political savvy and their ability to leverage their influence. Narottam's letter to the Omani Imam, which is often overlooked in mainstream histories, was a crucial factor in galvanizing Omani forces against the Portuguese.

The incident also highlights the importance of understanding the perspectives of marginalized communities in historical narratives. Mainstream histories often focus on the actions of powerful rulers and military leaders, neglecting the contributions of ordinary people. Narottam's story is a reminder that history is shaped by the actions of individuals from all walks of life. The rise of the Yaruba dynasty in Oman in the 17th century was a pivotal moment in the history of the region. The decades of internecine tribal wars had weakened Oman, leaving it vulnerable to external threats. Nasir bin Murshid, a charismatic leader from the Yaruba tribe, emerged as a unifying force, bringing together the disparate tribes under his banner.

Nasir bin Murshid's success lay in his ability to tap into the deep-seated resentment against the Portuguese presence in Oman. He skillfully framed the Portuguese as "infidel, beardless polytheists," who were exploiting the resources of the region and undermining the Islamic faith. His message resonated with the Omani tribes, who were eager to expel the Portuguese and restore their own sovereignty. Nasir bin Murshid's military campaigns against the Portuguese were marked by both successes and failures. His initial attempts to capture Portuguese forts were met with resistance, but he persevered, learning from his mistakes and refining his strategies. His capture of the forts at Ras al-Khaimah and Sur demonstrated his military prowess and his determination to drive the Portuguese out of Oman.

Nasir bin Murshid's alliance with the British East India Company was a strategic move that further strengthened his position. The British, eager to expand their own trade interests in the region, provided Nasir bin Murshid with military support and access to advanced weaponry. Nasir bin Murshid's legacy is that of a unifier and a liberator. He brought together the Omani tribes, ended decades of internal conflict, and laid the foundation for a powerful and independent Omani state. His military victories against the Portuguese marked a turning point in the history of the region, signaling the decline of Portuguese power and the rise of Omani influence.

The siege of Muscat in 1649 was a climactic event in the struggle between the Omanis and the Portuguese. Sultan bin Saif, Nasir bin Murshid's successor, inherited the task of capturing the last Portuguese stronghold in Oman. The Portuguese, aware of their precarious position, had fortified Muscat, turning it into a formidable fortress. They had deployed a large garrison and equipped the forts with cannons and other defensive weapons. Sultan bin Saif's forces faced a daunting challenge in trying to breach the

Portuguese defenses.

The siege was a protracted and bloody affair. The Omanis launched repeated assaults on the forts, but they were met with fierce resistance from the Portuguese. The Portuguese had erected towers on the mountains surrounding Muscat, from which they could rain down fire on the Omani troops. They had also deployed an ingenious system of "iron cradles" suspended from chains, which concealed musketeers who could fire upon the approaching Omanis. The Omanis, despite their numerical superiority, found themselves bogged down in a frustrating stalemate.

The tide of the battle turned unexpectedly due to a personal conflict between the Portuguese commandant of Muscat, Pareira, and a prominent Sindhi Bhatia merchant named Narottam. Pareira, infatuated with Narottam's daughter, demanded her hand in marriage. Narottam, horrified by the proposal, refused, citing religious and cultural differences. Pareira, enraged by Narottam's defiance, threatened to use force to compel him to comply.

Narottam, realizing the danger he and his family faced, devised a clever plan to buy time. He pretended to agree to the marriage proposal, but asked for a year to prepare for the wedding, citing the need to procure elaborate dresses and ornaments from India. Pareira, blinded by his desire, agreed to Narottam's request.
Narottam, having secured a reprieve, secretly wrote a letter to Sultan bin Saif, informing him of Pareira's vulnerability and urging him to press the attack. He also sent a message to Pareira, falsely claiming that his daughter was ready for the wedding and that he should come to his house to

finalize the arrangements.

Pareira, eager to claim his prize, fell into Narottam's trap. He left the fort with a small entourage and went to Narottam's house. As soon as he entered, Narottam's men overpowered him and his guards, taking them prisoner.

Narottam then sent a message to Sultan bin Saif, informing him of Pareira's capture. Sultan bin Saif, seizing the opportunity, launched a final assault on the forts. The Portuguese, demoralized by the loss of their commander and leaderless, were unable to mount an effective defense. The Omanis stormed the forts, capturing them after a fierce battle.

The fall of Muscat marked the end of Portuguese rule in Oman. The Omanis had finally achieved their goal of expelling the foreign invaders and restoring their independence. The victory was a testament to the courage and resilience of the Omani people and the leadership of Sultan bin Saif.

The expulsion of the Portuguese from Oman had far-reaching consequences. It marked the decline of Portuguese power in the Indian Ocean world and the rise of Omani influence. The Omanis, under the Yaruba dynasty, went on to establish a powerful maritime empire, controlling trade routes and establishing settlements along the coasts of East Africa and India.

The story of the siege of Muscat is a tale of courage, betrayal, and cunning. It highlights the role of personal relationships and individual actions in shaping historical events. It also underscores the importance of understanding the perspectives of marginalized communities in historical narratives. The story of Narottam, the Sindhi Bhatia merchant who played a pivotal role in the expulsion of the Portuguese, is a reminder that history is made not only by kings and generals but also by ordinary people.

CHAPTER SIX

THE ELEPHANT OF MAHARAJA JAYACHANDRA

The enduring stain of treachery, unjustly affixed to Maharaja Jayachandra, persists through the centuries, a testament to the power of narrative and the fragility of historical reputation. Among the luminaries of Hindu kingship, Jayachandra stands uniquely vilified, his name synonymous with betrayal, a legacy birthed from Chand Bardai's epic, the Prithviraj Raso. While Bardai's devotion to his master, Prithviraja Chahamana, is understandable, his denigration of Jayachandra casts a long shadow, obscuring the truth and disserving both monarchs.

Both Prithviraja and Jayachandra were formidable rulers, presiding over vast empires and commanding immense armies. Yet, both shared a critical flaw: a profound underestimation of the Turushka enemy, whose relentless incursions into northwestern Bharatavarsha had already carved out significant territories. This shared myopia, a failure to grasp the existential threat posed by the invaders, led to their downfall, culminating in the swift and devastating eclipse of Hindu political power in northern India within a mere two years. This tragic episode, detailed in my Invaders and Infidels: Book 1, underscores the pivotal role of strategic foresight in the face of implacable adversaries.

A counterfactual history, a mere whisper of what might have been, reveals the transformative potential of a united Hindu front. Had Prithviraja and Jayachandra set aside their animosity, forged an alliance against the Turushka menace, the course of India's history would have been irrevocably altered. Conversely, if Jayachandra had possessed a bard of Bardai's caliber, Prithviraja's legacy might have been similarly tarnished. The enduring power of narrative, its capacity to shape perceptions and solidify historical narratives, is starkly evident in this enduring vilification.

The "Jaichand" slur, a potent symbol of treachery, has effectively eclipsed Jayachandra's substantial contributions as a champion of Sanatana Dharma. The numerous inscriptions, both official and private, issued during his reign bear witness to his steadfast commitment to upholding the Dharma. These inscriptions, along with his patronage of scholars like Sri Harsha, author of the revered Naishadiya Caritam, one of the Pancha-Mahakavyas, reveal a ruler deeply invested in the intellectual and spiritual life of his kingdom.

The Gahadavala dynasty, under Jayachandra's leadership, emerged during a critical juncture in Hindu history, providing a century of stability and patronage. His defeat and death at the Battle of Chandawar, near Firozabad in Agra district, marked the end of this era. Muslim chroniclers, unanimous in their accounts, attest to Jayachandra's valor, the formidable size of his army, and the ferocity of the battle. Ibn Athir, for instance, describes Jayachandra as "the greatest king in India," whose territory stretched from the borders of China to Malwa, and from the sea to within ten days' journey of Lahore. While Ibn Athir's territorial claims may be exaggerated, they underscore the vastness of Jayachandra's empire and the power he wielded.

The Battle of Chandawar, as described by Ibn Athir, was a cataclysmic clash: "The Hindu prince had seven hundred elephants, and his men were said to amount to a million. There were many nobles in his army...When the two armies met there was great carnage; the infidels were sustained by their numbers...but in the end the infidels fled, and the faithful were victorious. The slaughter of the Hindus was immense; none were spared except women and children, and the carnage of the men went on until the earth was weary. Ninety elephants were captured, and of the rest some were killed, and some escaped. The Hindu king was slain..."

Following this decisive victory, Muhammad Ghori and Qutub-ud-din Aibak embarked on a campaign of iconoclasm in Varanasi, destroying a thousand temples within a week and erecting mosques in their place. The city's treasures were plundered, carried away on fourteen hundred camels, leaving Kashi forever transformed. The scars of this devastation remain visible even today, a testament to the enduring impact of religious zealotry.

Among the spoils of war were ninety elephants, one of which was a white elephant, a creature of profound significance to Jayachandra. This elephant held special reverence, rooted in the spiritual traditions of Sanatana and Bauddha Dharma. In the Sanatana tradition, the white elephant symbolizes Airavata, Indra's mount, while in the Buddhist tradition, it is associated with the birth of Buddha, who is believed to have reincarnated from white elephants descended from heaven.

Jayachandra's reverence for the white elephant stemmed from his initiation into Bauddha Dharma by the monk Srimitra. An inscription from around 1183 CE, found near Bodh Gaya, details how Jayachandra, a staunch Vaishnava, adopted Srimitra as his Diksha-Guru. This act of reverence, described as "with a pleasing heart and an indescribable hankering," reflects the accommodative spirit of his ancestors, who patronized and honored all panthas and margas, including Shaiva, Ganapatha, Shakta, and Bauddha. The white elephant, a rare and sacred animal, served as a tangible expression of Jayachandra's veneration for Srimitra and Bauddha Dharma. It was a symbol of his commitment to the inclusive and tolerant ethos of Sanatana Dharma, a testament to his respect for diverse spiritual paths.

The capture of this sacred elephant by the Turushkas naturally aroused their curiosity and wonder. Ibn Athir notes, "Among the elephants which were captured there was a white one. A person who saw it told me that when the elephants were brought before Shahabu-d din [Muhammad Ghori] and were ordered to salute, they all saluted except the white one."

The white elephant's refusal to salute the Turushka was not an act of defiance but a reflection of Jayachandra's principles. He had not trained the elephant to salute anyone, including himself, adhering to the tradition that sages do not salute kings. This act of principled resistance, a silent rebuke to the conquerors, underscores Jayachandra's commitment to his spiritual values.

To further understand the unfair nature of the Jaichand slur, we must delve into the political landscape of the time. Prithviraj Chahamana and Jayachandra were contemporaries, and their kingdoms shared a tumultuous border. Their rivalry, fueled by ambition and territorial disputes, was a constant source of conflict. The story of Samyogita's swayamvara, where Prithviraj abducted Jayachandra's daughter, further exacerbated their animosity. This personal vendetta, amplified by Chand Bardai's narrative, became the cornerstone of Jayachandra's vilification.

However, historical evidence suggests that Jayachandra's actions were not motivated by treachery but by strategic calculations. He faced a dual threat: the encroaching Turushkas and the rival Chahamanas. In his view, Prithviraj posed an immediate threat to his kingdom, while the Turushkas were a more distant concern. This strategic assessment, though flawed in hindsight, was not an act of betrayal but a calculated decision based on the information available to him.

The narrative of Jayachandra's treachery also ignores the

broader context of Hindu resistance against the Turushka invaders. While Prithviraj is celebrated for his valiant defense, Jayachandra's efforts to protect his kingdom and uphold Dharma are often overlooked. His patronage of scholars, his support for religious institutions, and his commitment to the welfare of his subjects are overshadowed by the single act of perceived betrayal.

The enduring legacy of the Jaichand slur highlights the power of narrative and the importance of critical historical analysis. Chand Bardai's epic, though a valuable literary work, should not be taken as an unbiased historical account. His portrayal of Jayachandra, driven by loyalty to his master, has perpetuated a distorted image of the king.

To reclaim Jayachandra's legacy, we must move beyond the confines of Bardai's narrative and examine the historical evidence with a critical eye. We must acknowledge his contributions as a patron of Dharma, a supporter of scholarship, and a valiant defender of his kingdom. We must also recognize the complexity of the political landscape in which he operated, understanding his decisions in the context of the threats he faced.

By doing so, we can restore Jayachandra's rightful place in history, not as a traitor but as a complex and multifaceted ruler who, like many others, made decisions that shaped the course of India's destiny. The white elephant's silent rebuke, a symbol of Jayachandra's principled resistance, serves as a poignant reminder of the king's commitment to his values, a commitment that deserves to be remembered and honored.

CHAPTER SEVEN

A VILLAGE SYSTEM IN SEVUNA

The concept of the self-sufficient village, a cornerstone of ancient Indian society, resonated through millennia, shaping the socio-political landscape of the subcontinent. This enduring institution, praised by both ancient Dharmasastra writers and 19th-century British officials, stood as a testament to the resilience and adaptability of Indian social structures. The essence of the village, as defined by Rishis Gautama and Bodhayana, lay in its moral foundation, a gathering place for righteous individuals. This seemingly simple definition encapsulated a profound truth, reflecting the ideal of a community built on ethical principles and social harmony.

Bodhayana, in his Dharmasutra, further elaborated on the ideal village, emphasizing the importance of resource availability, economic prosperity, social harmony, and security. "A righteous man shall seek to dwell in a village where fuel, water, fodder, sacred fuel, kusa grass, and garlands are plentiful. Access to all this must be easy, and many rich people should dwell in such a village. It ought to abound in industrious people, and where Aryas (virtuous, cultured, honest and honourable men) must form the majority. It should have a strong defence against robbers and other disturbers of peace." These guidelines underscore the holistic approach to village life, where material well-being was intertwined with moral and social values.

The ancient sages acknowledged that their tenets were rooted in the wisdom of their predecessors, suggesting that the concept of the self-governing village predated even their time. This continuity of tradition, spanning centuries, highlights the deep-seated nature of this institution within Indian society. The village, as a microcosm of the larger society, served as a vital link between the individual and the state, fostering a sense of community and shared responsibility.

The evolution of Sanatana civilization inevitably brought complexity and change to the village system. However, the core principles established by the Dharmasastra Rishis remained largely intact. The administrative mechanisms and functional aspects of the village evolved in response to changing times, adapting to the needs of different eras. This dynamic adaptation provides a unique lens through which to reconstruct the political and social history of Bharatavarsha from its civilizational dawn.

The resilience of these self-governing units, each functioning as a "separate little state in itself," contributed significantly to the preservation of Indian society through various upheavals. These upheavals, often triggered by foreign invasions or internal conflicts, rarely disrupted the fundamental structure of the village. The village, with its inherent self-sufficiency and communal spirit, acted as a buffer against external disruptions, ensuring the continuity of social and cultural traditions.

This continuity is evident in the administrative histories of various Hindu empires spanning nearly two millennia. Despite minor variations, the administrative structure of one Hindu empire closely mirrored that of another. For example, the 28 administrative departments mentioned in the annals of the Sena Empire (Bengal) were directly derived from the Arthasastra. Similarly, the Sevuna (Yadava) Empire, ruling from Devagiri, exhibited a comparable administrative setup.

The Sevuna Empire serves as an excellent case study to explore the Hindu village administrative system. Its selection also allows us to trace the origins of contemporary names, terminology, and functions that have survived to this day. Before delving into the specifics of the Sevuna Empire, however, it is essential to explore the undateable cradle of the Hindu village administrative setup.

The Grāma, or village, was consistently recognized as the fundamental unit of administration. Gautama and Bodhayana defined a village as a place where righteous men gathered. Kautilya, in his Arthasastra, defined a village as comprising 100-500 families, with well-defined boundaries and provisions for common defense against internal and external threats. The state could establish new villages in suitable locations, with housing sites allotted to various classes of people based on social status and family size.

While terminology varied, the core features of the village administrative system remained consistent across ancient India. The following provides a general overview:
* Grāma: The individual village, the smallest administrative unit.
* Saṅgrahaṇa: A group of ten villages.
* Kharvāṭikā: A group of two hundred villages.
* Drōṇamukha: A group of four hundred villages.
* Sthānīya: A group of eight hundred villages.
* Gulma: A unit of one thousand villages, subdivided into three groups: two hundred, three hundred, and five hundred.
* Dēśa: A group of one thousand villages. The modern meaning of Dēśa as "country" emerged later.
Each Grāma adhered to specific measurements, typically around two square miles. Its physical layout followed a strict plan of streets and roads, each named according to its function:
* Padya: Footpath. Width: Three cubits.
* Vīthi: Market street. The Kannada word Bīdi is derived from this. Width: Five cubits.
* Mārga: Road, transit road, avenue. Width: Ten cubits.
* Rājamārga: Royal road, highway. Width: Fifteen to thirty cubits.
An integral part of the village system was the Śāla, or resthouse, the precursor to the modern Dharma-Śāla. These resthouses, located between Grāmas, provided shelter and protection to travelers at night. The Śālādhipa,

the official in charge, acted as both a quasi-police officer and manager.

The village administrative setup was managed by a hierarchical structure of officials:

* Gōpa, grāmabhōjaka, grāmāṇi: The village headman, responsible for all village functions, including maintaining accounts.

* Śālādhipati: The village police chief.

* Officials in charge of Saṅgrahaṇas, Kharvāṭikās, and Drōṇamukhas.

* Sthānika: In charge of eight hundred villages (one Sthānīya).

* Samāhartā: The imperial official to whom the Sthānika reported, akin to a contemporary Finance Minister. The Samāhartā directly appointed the Sthānika.

This system emphasized a strict administrative hierarchy, with violations subject to swift punishment.

The enduring continuity of this system is evident in D.V.G.'s "Maisūrina divānarugaḷu" (The Divans of Mysore), which demonstrates how the British largely preserved the existing administrative structure. Villagers often regarded the Amaldar (Sthānika) as synonymous with the government. Similarly, Dr. S.L. Bhyrappa's "Tabbaliyu Neenaade Magane" provides a vivid account of the practical operation of this system and its impact on village life.

This overview of the ancient Indian village administrative setup provides a foundation for exploring its practical functioning in the Sevuna Empire, which was extinguished by Ala-ud-din Khalji in the early 14th century. The details reveal a sophisticated and enduring system of local governance, deeply rooted in the principles of self-sufficiency, communal responsibility, and ethical conduct.

To further understand the nuances of this system, we must delve into the specific context of the Sevuna Empire. The Sevunas, also known as the Yadavas of Devagiri, ruled a vast territory in the Deccan region, leaving behind a rich legacy of administrative practices and socio-cultural traditions. Their empire, characterized by a well-organized bureaucracy and a thriving economy, provides a valuable case study for examining the practical application of the ancient village system.

The Sevuna administration, like its predecessors, recognized the importance of local autonomy and self-governance. The village, as the fundamental unit of administration, played a crucial role in maintaining social order, collecting revenue, and providing essential services. The Sevuna rulers, while maintaining overall control, allowed villages to manage their own affairs, fostering a sense of ownership and responsibility among the villagers.

The Sevuna village administration was typically headed by a headman, known by various titles depending on the region. This headman, often chosen from among the prominent members of the village community, was responsible for maintaining law and order, collecting taxes, and resolving disputes. He was assisted by a council of elders, who provided advice and guidance on matters of local importance.

The Sevuna administration also maintained a network of officials at higher levels, overseeing groups of villages and ensuring the smooth functioning of the administrative machinery. These officials, appointed by the central government, acted as intermediaries between the village and the state, facilitating communication and ensuring the implementation of imperial policies.

The Sevuna Empire's economic prosperity was closely linked to the efficiency of its village administration. The villages, being the primary centers of agricultural production, contributed significantly to the state's revenue. The Sevuna rulers implemented various measures to promote agricultural development, including the construction of irrigation systems and the provision of agricultural loans.

The Sevuna administration also paid attention to the welfare of the villagers, providing essential services such as healthcare, education, and infrastructure development. The villages, with their inherent self-sufficiency and communal spirit, played a vital role in providing these services, supplementing the efforts of the central government.

The Sevuna Empire's village administration, therefore, represented a sophisticated and well-organized system of local governance, deeply rooted in the ancient traditions of India. This system, characterized by a balance between central control and local autonomy, contributed significantly to the stability and prosperity of the empire.

CHAPTER EIGHT

EDUCATION IN THE VIJAYNAGARA EMPIRE

The Vijayanagara Empire, true to its commitment to upholding the Pūravāda-maryāde, the preservation of ancient customs and traditions, fostered a unique and highly effective system of technical education. This system, deeply rooted in the guild and community structures of the time, emphasized the transmission of skills and knowledge through generations, ensuring the continuity of traditional crafts and professions.

Examining this system reveals the profounder aspects of the social structures often mislabeled as the "caste system." In the context of this discussion, we can refer to these structures as "professions," emphasizing the vocational nature of these social divisions. Skills, competence, excellence, and expertise in each profession were cultivated within families and communities, with knowledge passed down from father to son from an early age.

The training was rigorous, intensive, and prolonged, focusing not only on the mechanical aspects of the craft but also on the absorption of its spirit. This spirit, transcending mere technical proficiency, elevated the profession to a higher plane, fostering a deep sense of dedication and pride. This emphasis on the spirit of the profession, which cannot be taught in a classroom, distinguished the traditional system from modern educational approaches.

The ultimate goal of this training was the acquisition of mastery, a concept largely absent in contemporary educational paradigms. Today's generalist, often overwhelmed by the breadth of knowledge, struggles to discern the details, while the specialist, focused on a narrow field, loses sight of the interconnectedness of knowledge. The traditional system, in contrast, aimed to produce individuals with both depth and breadth, capable of mastering their craft while understanding its place within the larger societal context.

D.V.G., in his profile of Sivapicchai Mudaliar, provides a compelling illustration of this mastery. Sivapicchai, a mason by profession, possessed an extraordinary ability to detect minute discrepancies in the alignment of structures, correcting them with remarkable precision. This level of expertise, achieved through years of dedicated practice, reflects the high standards of craftsmanship prevalent in traditional Indian society.

Given this context, we can only imagine the quality and standard of professional and technical excellence that flourished in the Vijayanagara Empire. Foreign travelers, who visited the empire, left behind glowing accounts of its skilled artisans and craftsmen. The empire boasted a diverse range of professions, including architecture, sculpture, carpentry, smithy, gemology, weapon-making, ornament-making, and pottery.

Abdur Razak, in his description of Sri Krishnadevaraya's throne, highlights the exceptional craftsmanship of Vijayanagara artisans: "The throne, which was of an extraordinary size, was made of gold, and enriched with precious stones of extreme value; the whole workmanship was perfect in its delicacy and ingenuity. It is probable, that in all the kingdoms of the world, the art of inlaying precious stones is no where better understood than in this country." This description reveals the mastery of multiple crafts, including goldsmithing, gem-cutting, and inlay work.

The literary accomplishments of the Vijayanagara Empire are equally remarkable. The Rayas, known for their patronage of piety and literature, fostered a vibrant intellectual environment. Mahāmaṇḍalēśvaras, Nayakas, Palegars, and wealthy merchants vied with one another to support literary endeavors, leading to a flourishing of literary activity.

Literature in the Vijayanagara Empire can be broadly classified into two categories: sacred and secular. The empire made significant contributions to both categories.

One of the most notable contributions to sacred literature was Sāyanācārya's monumental commentaries on the Vedas. These commentaries, commissioned by the Rayas, remain invaluable resources for understanding Vedic texts.

The Rayas also encouraged the composition of works in Sanskrit and other Indian languages. Kumaravyasa's epic Karnāṭabhāratakathāmanjari blossomed under the patronage of Devaraya II. Telugu literature reached its golden age during the reign of the Rayas, with Sri Krishnadevaraya's Aṣṭa-diggajas becoming legendary.

Literary education in the empire received substantial support from aristocrats and merchants. Mahakavi Srinatha, in his works, extols the virtues of his numerous patrons. Agraharas, villages granted to learned Brahmins, served as centers of learning and literary activity. Temples and Mathas also received generous endowments, supporting scholars, poets, and artists.

The Vijayanagara court also witnessed the rise of individuals from humble backgrounds, who achieved prominence through their talent and dedication. The story of Kondoja, a barber who gained influence in the court, and used it to support the literary career of Rudrayya, a goldsmith poet, exemplifies this phenomenon.

The literary education and excellence of women in the Vijayanagara Empire is another remarkable aspect of its cultural history. Gangadevi, Bukkaraya's daughter-in-law, authored Madhurā-vijayam, a historical poem that has gained renewed attention in recent times. Tirumalamba

Devi's Varadāmbikāpariṇayam is also recognized as a significant literary work. Ramabhadramba, an Aṣṭāvadhāni proficient in three languages, composed the epic poem Raghunāthābhyudayam, a valuable historical source that also mentions the presence of numerous poetesses in her husband's court.

The educational system of the Vijayanagara Empire, characterized by its private nature and deep reverence for Saraswati, produced remarkable achievements in all fields of knowledge. It fostered a culture of learning for its own sake, transcending mere utilitarian considerations.

However, the system also served practical purposes, providing a constant supply of skilled individuals for the civil and military apparatus of the empire. The high demand for skilled labor led to rigorous training programs, ensuring that apprentices were well-prepared for their roles in society.

The legacy of this educational system is still visible in the literary corpus, architectural monuments, and artistic creations of the Vijayanagara era. The remnants at Hampi, the paintings at Lepakshi, Kanchi, and Thanjavur, and the numerous literary works stand as testaments to the system's success.

Even without deliberate state patronage, the system fostered a culture of excellence in all branches of learning. The deep reverence for Saraswati, combined with community values and a genuine love for knowledge, ensured the continuation of high standards in education.

To further delve into the intricacies of this system, we must examine the specific methods of knowledge transmission within guilds and communities. The guild system, prevalent in the Vijayanagara Empire, played a crucial role in maintaining quality control and ensuring the continuity of traditional crafts.

Guilds, often organized along professional lines, established standards for craftsmanship, regulated apprenticeship programs, and resolved disputes among members. They also played a vital role in protecting the interests of their members, negotiating with the government, and promoting trade.

Within guilds, knowledge was transmitted through a combination of formal and informal methods. Apprentices, typically young boys from the same community, began their training at an early age, learning the basics of their craft under the guidance of experienced masters.

The apprenticeship period was rigorous and prolonged, often lasting several years. During this time, apprentices learned not only the technical skills of their craft but also the ethical and social values associated with their profession.

The emphasis on practical training ensured that apprentices gained hands-on experience, mastering the techniques and nuances of their craft. They also learned to use the tools and materials of their trade, developing a deep understanding of their properties and applications.

Beyond technical skills, apprentices were also expected to absorb the spirit of their profession, developing a sense of dedication and pride in their work. This emphasis on the spirit of the profession, which transcended mere technical proficiency, distinguished the traditional system from modern educational approaches.

The community also played a vital role in supporting the educational process. Families and neighbors provided encouragement and support to apprentices, creating a nurturing environment for learning. Community events, such as festivals and religious ceremonies, provided opportunities for apprentices to showcase their skills and gain recognition for their work.

The Vijayanagara Empire's educational system, therefore, represented a holistic approach to learning, integrating technical skills, ethical values, and community support. This system, deeply rooted in the guild and community structures of the time, ensured the continuity of traditional crafts and professions, contributing to the empire's cultural and economic prosperity.

The enduring legacy of this system is evident in the rich cultural heritage of South India, which continues to inspire and influence generations of artists, craftsmen, and scholars.

CHAPTER NINE

The Forgotten Hindu History of Pakistan

Let us embark on a detailed exploration, weaving the threads of sacred geography, forgotten histories, and the enduring spirit of Sanatana Dharma into a grander narrative.

In the hushed cadence of the Ishavasya Upanishad, the profound declaration "ईशावास्य इदं सर्वं यत्किञ्चि जगत्या जगत्" reverberates through the ages, a timeless truth etched in the very fabric of existence. It proclaims that all that moves and breathes within the cosmos is imbued with the divine presence of Ishwara. This realization, a cornerstone of spiritual awakening, fosters a profound sense of detachment from the ephemeral allurements of the material world. It gently nudges the seeker towards the path of renunciation, urging "मा गृध: कस्यस्वद्धिधनम्," a gentle admonition against coveting the possessions of others. In these sixteen sacred syllables, we find the sanctification of all creation, a boundless embrace of divinity that transcends the limitations of space and time.

This sacred geography, this Punyabhoomi, finds its most cherished and enduring embodiment in the hallowed land of Bharatavarsha. Unlike the transient notions of "Fatherlands" that have risen and fallen throughout history, Bharatavarsha is revered as a nurturing mother, a Pavitrabhoomi, a Karmabhoomi, a Dharma-kshetra. The very essence of this sacred land is interwoven with the intricate tapestry of Hindu consciousness, a living testament to the enduring resonance of "ईशावास्यं इदं सर्वं." The countless Tirtha-Yatras, the sacred pilgrimages that punctuate the lives of countless devotees, serve as living proof of this profound spiritual connection. These journeys, undertaken with unwavering faith and devotion, are not merely physical movements across the land; they are spiritual odysseys, pathways to inner transformation and communion with the divine.

As an ancient poet eloquently proclaimed, his words echo through the corridors of time, "Let me be born as a tree, shrub, plant, or worm or pebble, but let me be born in Bharatavarsha and nowhere else." This unwavering reverence, this fervent celebration of the land's sanctity, echoes through the verses of slokas, the narratives of Puranas, and the injunctions of Dharmashastras, as aptly captured by Diana Eck's seminal work, "India: A Sacred Geography." The very soil of Bharatavarsha is imbued with a sacredness that transcends the mundane, a sanctity that permeates every aspect of life.

The grand Mahasankalpa of the Matsya Purana, a veritable atlas and almanac of ancient Bharatavarsha, stands as a testament to this sacred geography. Recited during the auspicious Kanyadanam ritual, it embodies an unbroken civilizational continuity, a thread that stretches back to the dawn of time. It meticulously catalogues the mountains, forests, rivers, islands, groves, kingdoms, pilgrimage spots, and great cities of Bharatavarsha, painting a vivid and intricate portrait of its vast and diverse expanse.

"अङ्ग वङ्ग कलङ्ग कश्मीर कंभोज कामरूप..." – a litany of fifty-six Deshas, each a jewel in the crown of Bharatavarsha, a testament to the intricate tapestry of its ancient geography. These regions, each with its unique cultural and historical significance, formed the very fabric of the land. From the heartland of Madhya Desha, the central core of the nation, to the western frontiers of Aparanta, the boundaries that faced the setting sun, from the northern reaches of Udeecya Desha, the lands that stretched towards the celestial pole, to the eastern expanse of Prachya Desha, the domains that embraced the rising sun, and the southern depths of Dakshinapatha, the regions that extended towards the southern ocean, the land was divided into five distinct regions, a classification echoed even by ancient Chinese scholars as the Five Indies. This shared understanding of the land's divisions speaks to a profound cultural exchange and a shared sense of geographical identity.

Geography and history, inextricably intertwined, shape and reshape each other, with geography serving as the very memory of a civilization. The loss of physical geography is, therefore, a profound loss of narrative memory, a severing of the threads that connect us to our past. The forgotten Hindu history of regions now encompassed by Pakistan, Afghanistan, and Bangladesh represents a poignant narrative loss for Bharatavarsha, a wound that continues to bleed.

The Vedic hymns, such as the evocative "इमं मे गङ्गे यमुने सरस्वति," resound with the names of rivers, many of which now flow through lands beyond Bharatavarsha's borders – the Indus, Raavi, Sutlej, Jhelum, and Chenab, the very lifeblood of the Panchanada Kshetra. These rivers, once integral to the spiritual and cultural landscape of Bharatavarsha, now flow through lands that have been severed from their ancestral roots. The names of rivers like Yavyavati, Gomati, Kubha, and Krumu have been altered, a subtle yet profound erasure of civilizational memory, a deliberate attempt to sever the connection to the past.

The fifty-six Deshas of the Mahasankalpa, the sixteen Mahajanapadas, and the countless Tirtha-Kshetras, like Aapagaa, Arjikiya, Bhiimaayaa-Sthanam, and Devika, stand as silent witnesses to the lost grandeur of Bharatavarsha. The loss of these sacred spaces is not merely geographical; it is a profound spiritual wound, a decimation of Sanatana civilization itself. These sacred sites, once vibrant centers of spiritual activity, now lie in ruins, their sanctity desecrated, their voices silenced.

The Panchangam, the Hindu calendar, serves as a poignant reminder of this loss. Once, it would have detailed the festivals and celebrations of Tirtha-Kshetras now beyond reach. The absence of this sacred geography in our present-day consciousness is a testament to the erasure of memory, a deliberate attempt to sever the connection to our past.

The deliberate alteration of names, the destruction of temples, and the obliteration of cultural symbols – these are the hallmarks of a history rewritten by conquest. The fall of Hampi, the transformation of the Pancha-Nada Kshetra, and the loss of Sindh are stark reminders of this erasure, of the systematic destruction of a civilization's heritage.

The Grand Route, a commercial and cultural artery that once connected the Caspian Sea to the borders of China, stands as a testament to the vibrant trade and cultural exchange that flourished in Bharatavarsha. From Pushkalavati to Takshashila, from Mulasthana to Haarahoora, these bustling centers of commerce and culture have been lost, their Sanatana past fading into oblivion. These cities, once vibrant hubs of economic and intellectual activity, now lie in ruins, their glory reduced to whispers in the wind.

The heroes of Bharatavarsha – Maharshi Panini, Acharya Chanakya, Ashvaghosha, Nagasena, Vasubandhu, Jivaka, and Charaka – stand in stark contrast to the conquerors who sought to erase their legacy. The loss of the Sama Veda and Atharva Veda branches, the destruction of literary works, and the suppression of Sanskrit learning represent a profound cultural impoverishment, a silencing of the voices of wisdom.

The resilience of the Sanatana spirit, however, shines through the reconquests of the Marathas and Maharaja Ranjit Singh. Yet, the continued destruction of temples and the rewriting of history serve as a stark reminder of the ongoing struggle to preserve the memory of Bharatavarsha's glorious past.

The teaching of chemistry by the grace of Allah in Pakistani textbooks, is a warning of what can happen when history is forgotten, when the threads of cultural memory are severed. Therefore, the preservation of the Hindu history of Pakistan is not merely a matter of academic interest; it is a civilizational imperative, a sacred duty to remember and honor the legacy of Bharatavarsha, to ensure that the voices of our ancestors continue to resonate through the ages.

CHAPTER TEN

THE SOMNATH TEMPLE

The Somnath Temple, standing majestically on the western coast of India, is more than just a religious edifice; it is a living chronicle of Bharat's tumultuous history, a testament to the nation's unwavering spirit in the face of repeated depredations. Much like the broader narrative of Bharatvarsha, Somnath's past is marked by cycles of destruction and reconstruction, a poignant reflection of the resilience that has defined the land for millennia.

The origins of the Somnath Temple are shrouded in the mists of time, intertwined with the rich tapestry of Indian mythology. Legends speak of its initial construction in gold by Somraj, the Moon God, a celestial being whose brilliance illuminates the night sky. This act of divine creation imbued the temple with an aura of sanctity from its very inception.

However, the temple's mythical origins do not end there. The legends continue, recounting its subsequent recreation in shimmering silver by Ravana, the mighty demon king of

Lanka. This act, though performed by a being associated with darkness, further solidified the temple's sacred status, demonstrating its ability to transcend the boundaries of good and evil.

Lord Krishna, an avatar of Vishnu, the preserver of the cosmos, is said to have rebuilt the temple in fragrant sandalwood, further enhancing its spiritual significance. This act of divine intervention cemented Somnath's place as a sacred site, a focal point for devotion and spiritual awakening.

Later, Bhimdeva, a ruler of Gujarat, is credited with constructing the temple in stone, marking a transition from mythical origins to documented history. This act of human endeavor, inspired by divine legends, solidified Somnath's physical presence, transforming it into a tangible symbol of devotion.

These mythical narratives, passed down through generations, serve not only to embellish the temple's antiquity but also to underscore its profound spiritual significance. The association with celestial beings and divine avatars elevates Somnath beyond a mere physical structure, transforming it into a conduit for cosmic energies and a focal point for devotion.

Historical records corroborate the temple's repeated desecration and reconstruction, painting a vivid picture of its tumultuous past. Over centuries, various Muslim monarchs, driven by a combination of greed, religious zeal, and a desire to assert their dominance, subjected Somnath to repeated acts of plunder and vandalism.

Mahmud Ghazni, the infamous Turkic conqueror, led a particularly devastating raid in the 11th century. His forces not only looted the temple's vast wealth but also massacred thousands of innocent pilgrims who had sought refuge within its sacred walls. The temple was set ablaze, its once-resplendent structure reduced to smoldering ruins.

Ghaznavi's attack was not merely a military conquest; it was a calculated assault on the heart of Hindu faith. His objective was to shatter the spiritual morale of the Hindu populace, to demonstrate the perceived impotence of their deities. However, despite the immense physical damage, Ghaznavi failed to extinguish the flame of devotion that burned brightly in the hearts of the people.

The temple's destruction ignited a fire of resistance within the Hindu community. Rulers from across Bharatvarsha rose to the challenge, vowing to restore Somnath to its former glory. Shri Vikramaditya of Ujjaini, the Vallabhi kings, Bhimadeva of Anhilawada, and Khangara, the king of Junagadh, are among the many who dedicated their resources and efforts to rebuilding the sacred site.

This cycle of demolition and reconstruction continued for centuries, a testament to the enduring struggle between forces of destruction and forces of creation. The temple became a symbol of resistance, an embodiment of the resilience that has enabled Bharat to withstand countless adversities. Each act of reconstruction was not merely a physical restoration; it was a reaffirmation of faith, a declaration that the spirit of Somnath could not be extinguished.

The temple that stands today is a testament to the vision and determination of Sardar Vallabhbhai Patel, the Iron Man of India. During his visit to Prabhas in 1947, Patel, deeply moved by the temple's ruined state, resolved to rebuild it. His unwavering determination and leadership galvanized the nation, transforming the dream of a resurgent Somnath into a tangible reality.

The mosque erected by Aurangzeb atop the temple ruins was relocated, paving the way for the restoration of the sacred site. The Jyotirling Pratishthan, performed by Dr. Rajendra Prasad on May 11, 1951, marked the culmination of Patel's vision, restoring Somnath to its rightful place as a beacon of Hindu faith.
The modern Somnath Temple, designed in the Chalukya style of temple architecture by the Sompara community under the auspices of Prabhashankar Sompura, is a masterpiece of craftsmanship. The honey-colored stone, adorned with intricate carvings, speaks volumes about the skill and artistry of Indian artisans.

The temple complex features well-maintained gardens, the ornate Digvijay Dwar gateway, intricate artwork on walls and ceilings, and the beautiful Sabha Mandap (Assembly Hall) and Nritya Mandap (Dance Hall). A statue of Sardar Vallabhbhai Patel stands at the main gate, a tribute to the man who made the temple's reconstruction possible.

The Somnath Temple's spiritual significance is further enhanced by its location at Triveni Sangam, the confluence of the holy rivers Kapila, Hiran, and Saraswati. This sacred confluence imbues the surroundings with an aura of tranquility and spirituality, making it an ideal location for meditation and contemplation.

Somnath is also revered as the place where Lord Krishna took his divine journey to Neejdham (his heavenly abode). His funeral rites were performed at Triveni Sangam, further sanctifying the site and adding to its spiritual aura.

Ancient Hindu texts, including the Rig Veda, Shiv Puran, Shreemad Bhagavad Geeta, and Skanda Purana, mention the Somnath Temple, attesting to its antiquity and importance. The Skanda Purana states that the original Somnath Temple was built some 7,99,25,105 years ago, highlighting its timeless significance.

The temple's construction is also associated with the legend of Daksha's curse on Chandra Deva (the Moon God). When Chandra Deva favored Rohini among his 27 wives (all daughters of Daksha), Daksha cursed him with Kshay (gradual degeneration). Lord Brahma advised Chandra Deva to worship Lord Shiva at Prabhas Teerth.

Following Brahma's advice, Chandra Deva performed rigorous penance, reciting the Mahamrityunjaya Mantra. Lord Shiva, pleased with his devotion, offered him refuge in his dreadlocks and partially revoked the curse. As a result, Chandra Deva would wax and wane, symbolizing the cyclical nature of time.

In gratitude, Chandra Deva built a beautiful temple in gold for Lord Shiva, naming it Somnath (Soma meaning moon). He also installed the first Jyotirlinga, Somnath Mahadev, and resolved to spend equal time with each of his 27 wives.

The Somnath Temple is shrouded in intriguing legends and scientific curiosities. The Jyotirlinga enshrined here is said to possess alchemic and radioactive properties, creating a magnetic field that causes it to levitate.

The Baan-Stambh (Arrow Pillar), erected on the seashore south of the temple, bears an inscription in Sanskrit stating that there is no landmass between the Somnath seashore and Antarctica. This geographical anomaly adds to the temple's mystique.

Every evening, a one-hour light and sound show at the Somnath Temple narrates the temple's history and significance, providing devotees with a captivating glimpse into its rich past.

The Somnath Temple, through its long and tumultuous history, has emerged as a symbol of enduring faith and resilience. Its story is a testament to the indomitable spirit of Bharat, a nation that has withstood countless adversities and emerged stronger than ever.

The repeated destruction and reconstruction of Somnath mirror the broader narrative of Bharatvarsha, a land that has faced numerous invasions and challenges throughout its history. Yet, despite these setbacks, the spirit of Bharat has never been extinguished. The people have always risen to the occasion, rebuilding their lives and their sacred spaces, reaffirming their faith and their commitment to their cultural heritage.

The Somnath Temple stands as a beacon of hope, a symbol of the enduring power of faith and the indomitable spirit of Bharat. Its story is an inspiration to all who face adversity, a reminder that even in the darkest of times, the human spirit can triumph.

BONUS FEATURES

These are limited pieces of information, often related to the everyday life of the reader, making them more enjoyable. (In this book's BONUS FEATURES, the reader will find stories and tales revolving around food.)

CHAPTER ELEVEN

BONUS FEATURE – THE POWER OF IDLI

The idly, a seemingly simple steamed rice cake, has achieved a remarkable feat, quietly conquering the world's culinary landscape while the spotlight remained fixated on technological advancements and corporate giants. This unassuming dish, with its cherubic appearance and unpretentious purity, has transcended borders and cultures, establishing itself as a global culinary phenomenon.

The idly's triumph stands in stark contrast to the aggressive marketing strategies employed by multinational fast-food chains. While these corporations invested millions in market research and elaborate entry strategies, the idly simply relied on its inherent qualities to win over hearts and palates. The Indian "market," with its discerning taste buds and deep-rooted culinary traditions, decisively rejected the original menus of these fast-food giants, forcing them to adapt and "Indianize" their offerings.

The idly, on the other hand, needed no such adaptations. It traveled the world in its purest form, carried by the winds of cultural exchange and the universal language of good food. Its blandness, often perceived as a lack of flavor, is in fact its greatest strength. The idly is harmless, easily digestible, and versatile, capable of being paired with a wide range of accompaniments.

The idly's preparation requires no specialized culinary expertise, making it accessible to all. Its simplicity, however, does not diminish its appeal. The idly is irresistible, a culinary delight that transcends social and cultural barriers.

Despite its global reach, the idly's journey to international stardom is a relatively recent phenomenon. Just a century ago, the idly was largely confined to the Tamil-speaking regions of South India. This limited reach is intriguing, given the idly's Vedic origins, a fact that speaks to the dish's ancient roots and enduring appeal.

Sri Sediyapu Krishna Bhatta, a renowned scholar and linguist, has meticulously traced the idly's history in his insightful Kannada essay, "iḍliya itihāsa." His exploration, marked by rigorous reasoning and multidisciplinary scholarship, sheds light on the idly's etymological journey and its cultural evolution.
Bhatta's research reveals that the word "idly" is derived from the ancient Sanskrit word "iṇdra," which refers to a utensil used in yajnas (fire sacrifices). This "iṇdra" bears

a striking resemblance to the modern idly steamer, highlighting the enduring connection between ancient traditions and contemporary culinary practices.

The idly's presence in South India during the early medieval period is evidenced by the mention of "iḍḍalige" in the 9th-century Kannada work "vaḍḍārādhane." Bhatta also unearths a verse from the 10th-11th century Ayurvedic treatise "cakradattā saṃhita" that describes the preparation of "inḍari" using black gram and the root of the godhāpadī plant. This verse highlights the idly's medicinal properties and its use in traditional healing practices.

The author of "cakradattā saṃhita," Chakrapanidatta, lived in the Gauda-Desha (Bengal), suggesting that the idly's influence extended beyond South India during this period. Bhatta's research also reveals the existence of a sweet dish called "inḍri" prepared by the Gauda Saraswat Brahmin community in 20th-century coastal Karnataka. This dish, prepared using the same utensil and method as the idly, further reinforces the idly's ancient roots and its connection to various regional culinary traditions.

Bhatta concludes his exploration by explaining the phonetic transformation of "inḍra" into "idly." He suggests that "inḍrī" was the original phonetic form of the dish, which later became "iḍḍali" in Kannada. The additional "ḍ" sound was eventually dropped, resulting in the current form, "iḍli" or "idly."

The idly's journey from obscurity to widespread popularity in the Tamil-speaking regions of South India is closely intertwined with the advent of Indian Railways and the entrepreneurial spirit of the Palghat Iyers. The introduction of railways by the British in the 19th century transformed the socio-economic landscape of India, facilitating travel and trade across vast distances. In South India, the Tamil-speaking regions witnessed the most extensive rail networks, leading to increased mobility and cultural exchange.

The railways also created a demand for convenient and hygienic food options for travelers, particularly for the Brahmin community, who adhered to strict dietary restrictions. Palghat Iyers, known for their culinary skills and entrepreneurial spirit, seized this opportunity, establishing restaurants at railway stations across the Tamil region.

They discovered the idly, a dish that perfectly met the needs of travelers: it was easily digestible, versatile, and could be prepared quickly. The idly's Vedic origins and its connection to yajnas further appealed to the Brahmin community, who valued tradition and ritual.

The Palghat Iyers adapted the traditional "iṇḍra" utensil to prepare idlies, creating a portable and convenient food option for travelers. The idly's popularity quickly spread, becoming a staple at railway stations and beyond.

The idly's success was not merely a matter of convenience; it was also a testament to its inherent appeal. The Tamil populace, who had traditionally relied on leftovers for breakfast, readily embraced the idly, abandoning their old habits in favor of this new culinary delight.

The idly's popularity soared, transcending regional boundaries and social classes. It became a staple in restaurants across South India, and its fame eventually spread to other parts of the world.
The idly's global conquest is a testament to its soft power, its ability to influence and persuade through cultural exchange and culinary diplomacy. The idly has become a culinary ambassador for South India, introducing its flavors and traditions to a global audience.

The idly's success highlights the power of food as a cultural bridge, connecting people across continents and cultures. The idly's simple yet versatile nature has allowed it to adapt to various culinary traditions, becoming a part of the global culinary landscape.

The idly's story is a reminder that cultural exchange is not always driven by corporate marketing campaigns or political agendas. Sometimes, it is the simple things, like a humble steamed rice cake, that have the power to unite people and transcend borders.

The idly's triumph is a celebration of Indian culinary heritage, a testament to the enduring appeal of traditional foods in a globalized world. It is a reminder that cultural exchange is a two-way street, and that even in the age of globalization, local traditions and flavors can thrive and influence the world.

The idly's journey from ancient Vedic rituals to global culinary stardom is a testament to its enduring appeal and its ability to adapt and evolve. It is a story of cultural exchange, culinary innovation, and the power of food to connect people across borders and cultures. The idly, in its unassuming simplicity, has achieved a remarkable feat, quietly conquering the world's palate and establishing itself as a true culinary ambassador for India.

CHAPTER TWELVE

BONUS FEATURE – THE STORY OF SAMBHAR

South Indian cuisine, a vibrant tapestry of flavors and traditions, is inextricably linked to the ubiquitous presence of dishes like idli and sambar, or sambar and rice. These culinary pairings, deeply ingrained in the daily lives of South Indians, reflect the region's rich cultural heritage and its diverse culinary landscape. Each state in the South, with its unique preferences and environmental adaptations, prepares these dishes with subtle yet distinctive variations, creating a symphony of flavors that resonates with its people.

The genesis of sambar, a lentil-based vegetable stew, is shrouded in an intriguing tale that intertwines the culinary traditions of the Marathas and the South Indians. During the Maratha rule in Tanjore, King Sambhoji, a renowned cook, was particularly fond of his amti, a lentil soup flavored with kokum, a tart fruit imported from the Maratha homeland. However, on a particular day, the kokum supply was depleted, leaving the king's kitchen in a predicament.

As Sambhoji prepared to cook, his minions trembled in fear, dreading the task of informing him about the missing ingredient. A clever Vidushak, who had been appointed sous chef for the day, devised a solution. He whispered to the king that the locals used tamarind pulp, in small quantities, to achieve a similar sourness in their curries. Intrigued, Sambhoji decided to experiment with this variation.

He prepared a dish using tuvar dal, vegetables, spices, and tamarind pulp, and presented it to his court. The courtiers, faced with the king's culinary prowess, unanimously declared the dish an outstanding preparation. Thus, Sambhoji's amti, which eventually evolved into sambar, was born.

However, the preparation of sambar also became a point of contention between the Tanjoreans and the Pattars of Kerala. The Tanjoreans, known as "easterners" to the Pattars, were perceived as different, leading to social divisions. The Pattars, for instance, were hesitant to give their daughters in marriage to Tanjore families, fearing ill-treatment. However, they welcomed Tanjore daughters-in-law, recognizing their smartness and acumen in managing households.

The Tanjoreans frequently prepared vettal kuzhambu, a tamarind-based curry, as dal was often expensive for families relying on rituals and temple offerings. A small portion of dal, considered auspicious, would be served on the corner of a banana leaf, while the rice was mixed with the tamarind-based kuzhambu, thickened with rice powder and spices.

Pitlai, another dish influenced by Maratha cuisine, was reserved for festive occasions. Similarly, puli kuthina koottu, a thick stew made with various vegetables and tamarind pulp, was a staple in village homes. The basic recipe involved sautéing chana dal, red chilies, coriander seeds, asafoetida, and curry leaves, followed by the addition of ground coconut. The variation lay in the choice of raw or roasted coconut and the use of chana dal or urad dal, with a few grains of sesame added.

Rasavangi, another dish with Maratha influence, featured the same basic spices but included soaked grams like kondai kadalai or karamani. The non-Brahmins in Tanjore used a ready-made spice powder, called malli powder, for their curries. This powder, a blend of red chili and coriander seeds, was also used in meat dishes.

The Brahmin community, recognizing the convenience of spice powders, adopted this concept, particularly as their members migrated to cities like Chennai, Mumbai, Pune, and Delhi. The lack of fresh coconut in these urban centers further fueled the adoption of spice powders. It is important to note that until the arrival of the Nairs with their excess baggage of coconuts, Marathis and Gujaratis traditionally used copra, not fresh coconut.

In Kerala, coconut is an indispensable ingredient, used in both sweet and savory dishes. The sambar, introduced by migrant Pattars from Tanjore, was adapted to incorporate coconut. The ground spice paste with coconut, roasted coriander seeds, chana dal, and red chili remains the base for sambar in Kerala homes. The inclusion of coconut milk, a taste adopted from the local Namboodiris, further distinguishes Kerala sambar.

Karnataka has a unique approach to sambar preparation. They prepare a vegetable stew with a coarsely ground paste of pepper, coriander, cumin, red chili, dal, and coconut or copra. The curry is made watery, and after cooking, the liquid that floats is used as rasam, while the thicker portion is eaten as sambar. While this practice may be contested, it is typical of the Mandayam and Hebbar Iyengars. Their other sambar preparations include a dash of cinnamon and clove, a flavor profile also found in their famous Bisi Bela Huli baath. Authentic Bisi bela consists of tuvar dal, rice, tamarind, spices, and onions, with the addition of vegetables being a later development.

Andhra Pradesh, influenced by Chennai, has adopted sambar, but their culinary preferences lean towards various dry and wet chutneys and powders, followed by saaru or rasam. Pappu saaru, made with tuvar or moong dal, onions, tamarind pulp, red chili and coriander powder, asafoetida, and a seasoning of mustard and fenugreek seeds and curry leaves, is their main curry. The addition of tomatoes, after their introduction to Indian cuisine, has become a common practice in some families.

The use of ready-made sambar powder has gained immense popularity in many homes. Families were once meticulous about the proportion of ingredients and the grinding process, often opting for specific flour mills to ensure the purity of the powder.

Thus, sambar assumes numerous forms across the four states of South India, each reflecting the region's diverse culinary heritage and its people's unique preferences. The evolution of sambar, from its origins in the Maratha kitchen to its diverse adaptations across South India, highlights the dynamic interplay of cultural influences and culinary innovation.

The story of sambar is also a story of migration, adaptation, and the constant negotiation between tradition and change. The Marathas, through their rule in Tanjore, introduced new culinary techniques and ingredients, which were then adapted and integrated into the local cuisine. The migration of Brahmins to urban centers and to Kerala also played a crucial role in the spread and evolution of sambar.

The availability of ingredients and the changing socio-economic conditions also influenced the preparation of sambar. The use of tamarind pulp instead of kokum, the adoption of spice powders, and the integration of coconut milk reflect the resourcefulness and adaptability of South Indian cooks.
The variations in sambar preparation also highlight the regional differences in taste preferences. The Tanjoreans' preference for vettal kuzhambu, the Keralites' love for coconut, the Kannadigas' unique sambar-rasam combination, and the Andhras' fondness for chutneys and powders all contribute to the rich tapestry of South Indian cuisine.

The story of sambar is not just about a dish; it is a story

about the people who created it, the cultures that shaped it, and the traditions that continue to evolve. It is a testament to the enduring power of food to connect people, to bridge cultural divides, and to tell the story of a region's history and its people's lives.

The sambar, in its many avatars, continues to be an integral part of South Indian cuisine, a symbol of the region's culinary heritage and its people's enduring love for good food. It is a dish that transcends generations, connecting the past to the present and ensuring that the flavors of South India continue to tantalize taste buds for years to come.

CHAPTER THIRTEEN

BONUS FEATURE: THE ICONIC VADA PAV !

The Vada Pav, a culinary emblem of Mumbai, transcends its status as a mere snack; it embodies the very essence of the city's dynamic street culture, its entrepreneurial spirit, and its remarkable ability to transform humble ingredients into a gastronomic sensation. This iconic dish, born from the socio-political ferment of the 1960s, has become a symbol of Mumbai's resilience, its adaptability, and its enduring love for local flavors.

The story of the Vada Pav is not merely a tale of food; it's a narrative deeply intertwined with the city's history, its social fabric, and its economic evolution. It's a story that reflects the aspirations and struggles of ordinary Mumbaikars, their ingenuity, and their unwavering spirit.

Before delving into the Vada Pav's origins, it's essential to acknowledge the linguistic echoes of the Portuguese era.

The terms "batata" (potato) and "pav" (bread) bear testament to the Portuguese influence on the Indian coast. However, while they introduced these fundamental ingredients, the creation of the Vada Pav was a uniquely Indian innovation, a testament to the country's culinary creativity.

The credit for this iconic snack belongs to Ashok Vaidya, a visionary who, in the mid-1960s, recognized the potential of combining the simple elements of potato and bread into a satisfying and affordable meal. His stall, strategically located outside Dadar Station, a bustling transportation hub, catered to the thousands of textile mill workers who traversed the city daily.

Vaidya's initial offerings included vada and poha, alongside a stall selling omelette pav. One day, driven by a spark of inspiration, he experimented by placing a vada between a pav, adding a dash of chutney for flavor. This simple experiment, born out of necessity and ingenuity, resulted in the creation of the Vada Pav, a snack that quickly captured the hearts and palates of the city's working class.

The 1970s and 1980s were a period of significant socio-political upheaval in Mumbai, marked by numerous strikes and the eventual closure of many textile mills. This economic downturn, while devastating for many, also created a fertile ground for entrepreneurial ventures. Former mill workers, seeking new avenues for livelihood, were encouraged by the prevailing political climate to establish their own Vada Pav stalls.
This proliferation of Vada Pav vendors contributed to the snack's exponential rise in popularity. It became the

quintessential street food of the working class, offering a convenient, affordable, and filling meal option. Its appeal lay in its simplicity: it was easy to prepare, inexpensive, and could be consumed on the go, a crucial factor for those navigating the city's crowded local trains.

The arrival of American fast-food chains like McDonald's in the 1990s posed a potential threat to the Vada Pav's dominance. However, the Vada Pav's unique character and adaptability allowed it to withstand this challenge. McDonald's, with its standardized recipes and mechanized production, offered a uniform taste experience, a stark contrast to the Vada Pav's diverse flavors and regional variations.

Vada Pav vendors, with their individual recipes and secret ingredients, catered to the diverse palates of the Indian population. This emphasis on individuality and variety resonated with Indian consumers, who appreciated the nuanced flavors and regional adaptations offered by local vendors. McDonald's, with its one-size-fits-all approach, failed to capture the hearts and taste buds of Mumbai's street food enthusiasts.

In the year 2000, Mumbai-based entrepreneur Dheeraj Gupta recognized the economic potential of the Vada Pav and launched the "JumboKing" chain. Marketed as the "Indian Burger," JumboKing quickly expanded, establishing numerous outlets across Mumbai. This success highlighted the Vada Pav's enduring appeal and its ability to adapt to modern business models.

The Vada Pav's popularity has also inspired the creation of numerous other Vada Pav chains across India, each offering its own unique variations and interpretations of the classic snack. This proliferation of Vada Pav outlets further underscores its widespread acceptance and its status as a national culinary treasure.

In 2015, director Aalambayan Siddharth released a documentary, "Vada Pav Inc.," which paid tribute to Ashok Vaidya and his contribution to Mumbai's culinary heritage. This documentary helped to solidify Vaidya's legacy and ensure that his story would be passed on to future generations.

Ashok Vaidya passed away in 1998, but his legacy lives on through his son, Narendra, who continues to run the family's Vada Pav stall outside Dadar station. This enduring presence serves as a testament to the Vada Pav's enduring appeal and its connection to the city's history.

The Vada Pav, which first gained popularity over 50 years ago, continues to hold a special place in the hearts of people across Maharashtra and beyond. Its simple yet satisfying combination of flavors, its affordability, and its convenience have made it a staple of Indian street food.

The humble Vada Pav has traveled to numerous cities and towns, each offering its own variations and secret ingredients. This adaptability has contributed to its widespread appeal, making it a beloved snack across diverse regions.

August 23 is celebrated as World Vada Pav Day, a fitting tribute to this iconic Indian snack. The Vada Pav has created a fan base that spans generations and social classes, uniting people from all walks of life. From film stars and cricketers to politicians and daily wage laborers, the Vada Pav is a common denominator, a shared culinary experience that transcends social and economic barriers.

Ashok Vaidya's invention, the Vada Pav, has become more than just a snack; it's a symbol of Mumbai's spirit, its resilience, and its ability to create something extraordinary from simple ingredients. It's a testament to the power of local flavors and the enduring appeal of street food.

The Vada Pav's story is also a story of entrepreneurship and innovation. Ashok Vaidya's ability to recognize a need and create a solution, his willingness to experiment and adapt, and his dedication to providing a quality product have all contributed to the Vada Pav's success.

The Vada Pav's journey from a humble street stall to a national culinary icon is a testament to its enduring appeal and its ability to connect people across diverse backgrounds. It's a reminder that even the simplest of dishes can have a profound impact on a city's culture and its people's lives. The Vada Pav, in its unassuming simplicity, has become a symbol of Mumbai, a culinary ambassador that continues to delight and unite people across India and beyond.

CHAPTER FOURTEEN

BONUS FEATURE - BUTTER CHICKEN - A CREATIVE ADVENTURE

The allure of Butter Chicken, or Murgh Makhani as it's known in Hindi, extends far beyond the borders of India, captivating palates across the globe. This iconic dish, a symphony of creamy richness and aromatic spices, has become a culinary ambassador for Indian cuisine, its popularity rivaled by few other curries. Yet, despite its widespread acclaim, the humble origins of Butter Chicken remain shrouded in a veil of culinary lore, a tale that intertwines with the tumultuous history of the Indian subcontinent.

The story of Butter Chicken begins in pre-partition India, a time when culinary innovation flourished in the bustling streets of Peshawar, a city now located in Pakistan. At the heart of this narrative lies a small, unassuming restaurant named Mukhey Da Dhaba, owned by the venerable Mokha Singh. Within the walls of this dhaba, a young and ambitious worker named Kundan Lal Gujral was about to embark on a culinary journey that would forever change the landscape of Indian cuisine.

Gujral, endowed with a creative mind and a penchant for experimentation, was the mastermind behind the invention of Tandoori Chicken, a dish that would soon become a global sensation. His innovative technique of roasting chicken in a tandoor, a traditional clay oven, imparted a unique smoky flavor and tender texture that captivated the taste buds of patrons.

As time passed, Mokha Singh's health deteriorated, leading him to sell his beloved dhaba to Gujral, who renamed it Moti Mahal. Gujral, now the proprietor of his own establishment, faced a challenge: the tandoori chicken hanging on skewers tended to dry out throughout the day, losing its succulent appeal. Driven by a desire to minimize waste and offer his customers a consistently delectable experience, Gujral conceived a brilliant solution.

He envisioned a rich, creamy, and aromatic tomato-based gravy, infused with butter and spices, into which he could immerse the leftover tandoori chicken pieces. This ingenious idea not only prevented the chicken from drying out but also transformed it into a new culinary creation, a dish that was even more flavorful and tender than its predecessor. Thus, Butter Chicken was born, a serendipitous invention that emerged from a blend of practicality and culinary creativity.

In 1947, the partition of India and Pakistan forced Gujral to relocate to Delhi, India, a city renowned for its rich Mughlai culinary heritage. Undeterred by the upheaval, Gujral established Moti Mahal Deluxe in Daryaganj, a small restaurant that would eventually blossom into a chain of branches across India.

Today, 70 years later, Moti Mahal Deluxe stands as a testament to Gujral's culinary legacy, its branches managed by his grandson, Monish. The restaurant's Butter Chicken remains its signature dish, a culinary masterpiece that embodies the perfect balance of velvety texture and tangy flavor.

Monish Gujral, the custodian of his grandfather's culinary legacy, maintains that no other Butter Chicken can compare to the authentic Moti Mahal version. He attributes the dish's enduring popularity to its meticulous preparation, the careful selection of ingredients, and the unwavering adherence to the original recipe.

The beauty of Moti Mahal's Butter Chicken lies in its subtle nuances, the delicate interplay of flavors that avoids the pitfalls of excessive spiciness or cloying sweetness. Achieving this delicate balance requires a deep understanding of the ingredients and a mastery of the cooking techniques.

While many home cooks attempt to replicate the Moti Mahal experience, achieving the authentic taste requires a level of precision and expertise that is often elusive. The measurement of ingredients and the adherence to the traditional cooking procedures are crucial for replicating the dish's signature flavor.

Butter Chicken, in its essence, is a dish that embodies the spirit of Indian cuisine, a harmonious blend of tradition and innovation. Its story is a testament to the power of culinary creativity, the ability to transform humble ingredients into a gastronomic masterpiece.

The dish's journey from a small dhaba in Peshawar to the tables of restaurants across the globe is a reflection of its universal appeal, its ability to transcend cultural boundaries and captivate palates worldwide.

Butter chicken has also seen many variations. Some include the use of cashew paste to thicken the gravy, some use more cream, some use less. Every chef, every home cook, adds a little bit of their own personality to the dish. This makes it more than just a recipe; it's a living, breathing part of the culinary world.

The evolution of Butter Chicken also reflects the changing culinary landscape of India. As the country embraced globalization, the dish adapted to cater to diverse tastes and preferences. However, the core essence of Butter Chicken, its rich, creamy texture and its aromatic blend of spices, has remained unchanged.

The story of Butter Chicken is not just about a dish; it's a story about the people who created it, the cultures that shaped it, and the traditions that continue to evolve. It's a testament to the enduring power of food to connect people, to bridge cultural divides, and to tell the story of a nation's history and its people's lives.

The influence of the Mughlai cuisine, which was already very popular in Delhi, helped in further refining the butter chicken. The use of rich ingredients like cream, butter, and nuts, which were hallmarks of Mughlai cooking, gave the butter chicken its signature richness and flavor.

The partition of India and Pakistan, a tragic event in the history of the subcontinent, also played a role in the spread of Butter Chicken. As people migrated across the newly formed borders, they carried with them their culinary traditions, including the recipe for Butter Chicken.

The dish's journey from Peshawar to Delhi, and then to the rest of the world, is a testament to its resilience and its ability to adapt to changing circumstances. It's a story of culinary innovation, cultural exchange, and the enduring power of food to transcend borders.

Butter chicken has also become a symbol of Indian hospitality, a dish that is often served to guests as a gesture of warmth and welcome. Its rich, creamy texture and its aromatic blend of spices make it a crowd-pleaser, a dish that is sure to satisfy even the most discerning palate.

The dish's popularity has also led to the creation of numerous variations, each reflecting the regional preferences and culinary traditions of the area where it is prepared. From the spicy versions found in North India to the sweeter versions found in South India, Butter Chicken has adapted to cater to diverse tastes and preferences.

The evolution of Butter Chicken also reflects the changing dietary habits of Indians. As the country has become more prosperous, there has been a shift towards richer and more indulgent foods. Butter Chicken, with its creamy texture and its rich flavor, has become a symbol of this changing culinary landscape.

The story of Butter Chicken is a reminder that food is not just about sustenance; it's also about culture, history, and identity. It's a story that connects us to our past, our present, and our future. And it's a story that continues to be written, with every new variation and every new person who discovers its deliciousness.

CHAPTER FIFTEEN

BONUS FEATURE - THE SAMOSA STORY

The humble samosa, often relegated to the status of a simple street snack, holds within its crisp, golden embrace a narrative far grander than its unassuming appearance suggests. It is not merely a culinary delight; it is a historical artifact, a testament to the enduring power of cultural exchange, and a profound illustration of the fluidity of identity in a world shaped by migration and interaction. To bite into a samosa is to embark on a journey through millennia, traversing continents and cultures, and ultimately, to understand that the very notion of a static, nationally defined identity is as fragile as the deep-fried crust that envelops its savory heart.

The sensation of sinking one's teeth into the soft, yielding center of a samosa is a sensory explosion, a symphony of flavors that unfold across the palate. But more than just taste, it is the taste of history, the embodiment of India's very essence – a nation forged from the confluence of diverse peoples, traditions, and influences. The samosa is a tangible representation of this dynamic process, a culinary chronicle of the great migrations and interactions that have shaped the Indian subcontinent.

Contrary to popular belief, the samosa's origins lie not within the borders of modern-day India, but thousands of miles away, in the ancient empires that flourished on the Iranian plateau. Here, at the dawn of civilization, the seeds of the samosa were sown, nurtured by the culinary traditions of the Persian people. While the precise moment of its creation remains shrouded in the mists of time, the very name, "sanbosag," bears witness to its Persian roots.

The first literary mention of the samosa comes from the pen of the 11th-century Persian historian Abul-Fazl Beyhaqi. In his writings, he describes a delicate pastry, a culinary jewel served as a snack in the opulent courts of the mighty Ghaznavid empire. This early iteration of the samosa was a refined creation, a testament to the culinary artistry of the time. Thin, crisp pastry enveloped a filling of minced meats, nuts, and dried fruits, a harmonious blend of sweet and savory flavors.

However, the samosa's journey was far from over. It was destined to embark on an epic migration, following the footsteps of countless peoples who had traversed the ancient trade routes that connected Persia to India. This journey, mirroring the path taken by the Aryans millennia earlier, led through Central Asia, across the formidable mountain ranges of present-day Afghanistan, and finally, into the fertile plains of the Indian subcontinent.

The armies of the Mamluks, Tamerlane, and the Mughals, who followed in the wake of these earlier migrations, further cemented the samosa's place in the culinary landscape of India. Each wave of conquerors and settlers brought with them their own cultural baggage, contributing to the rich tapestry of Indian society and, inevitably, influencing the evolution of the samosa.

As the samosa journeyed eastward, it underwent a profound transformation, shedding its refined, courtly persona and adopting a more rustic, utilitarian form. By the time it reached the regions of modern-day Tajikistan and Uzbekistan, it had become, in the words of Professor Pushpesh Pant, a renowned expert on Indian cuisine, "a crude peasant dish." The delicate snack of the Persian courts had morphed into a hearty, high-calorie staple, a sustenance for shepherds and travelers.

While retaining its distinctive triangular shape and its fried preparation, the samosa's filling underwent a significant change. The exotic nuts and fruits of its Persian origins were replaced by coarsely chopped goat or lamb, seasoned simply with onions and salt. This transformation reflected the practical needs of a nomadic lifestyle, where sustenance and portability were paramount.

The samosa's arrival in the Indian subcontinent marked a pivotal moment in its evolution. Here, it found fertile ground for adaptation and innovation, becoming what Professor Pant aptly describes as the ultimate "syncretic dish," a fusion of cultures and culinary traditions. "I think the samosa tells you how influences, culinary and otherwise, have come across to us," he says, "and how India has adopted them, adapted them to its own requirements and milieu, and transformed them totally."

India's embrace of the samosa was characterized by a spirit of inclusivity and creativity. Local spices, such as coriander, pepper, caraway seeds, and ginger, were incorporated into the filling, adding depth and complexity to its flavor profile. The filling itself underwent a significant shift, with vegetables gradually replacing meat, reflecting the growing influence of vegetarianism within Indian society.

The arrival of the Portuguese in the 16th century brought about another transformative moment in the samosa's history. The introduction of potatoes and green chilies from the New World revolutionized Indian cuisine, and the samosa was no exception. These new ingredients, now considered quintessential components of the Indian samosa, became integral to its identity.

The samosa's journey did not end with its arrival in India. Over centuries, it continued to evolve, adapting to the diverse regional tastes and preferences of the subcontinent. From the monstrous, meal-sized samosas of some regions to the delicate, cocktail-sized versions served at upscale gatherings, the samosa's versatility knew no bounds.

The "lukhmi" of Hyderabad, a thin, crisp pastry filled with minced meat and peas, bears witness to the enduring influence of the courtly samosas described by the 14th-century Moroccan traveler Ibn Battuta. In Punjab, the addition of paneer, fresh Indian cheese, has become a hallmark of the local samosa, while in other parts of India, this innovation is met with skepticism.

The samosa's adaptability extends beyond its filling, encompassing even its cooking techniques. While the classic fried samosa remains the most popular, baked and steamed versions have emerged, catering to the health-conscious and adventurous palates. However, as Professor Pant argues, the absence of oil in steamed samosas compromises the development of flavors, highlighting the importance of traditional cooking methods.

The samosa's journey did not end in India. It embarked on a new phase of its global odyssey, spreading to far-flung corners of the world through the agency of the British Empire and the Indian diaspora. The British, who developed a fondness for the samosa during their colonial rule, introduced it to their vast network of colonies, alongside other Indian innovations such as shampoo, bungalows, verandas, and pyjamas.

The Indian diaspora, driven by economic opportunities and social mobility, carried the samosa with them as they settled in new lands. Today, the samosa can be found in virtually every corner of the globe, a testament to its enduring appeal and its ability to transcend cultural boundaries.

The samosa's global journey is a powerful reminder of the interconnectedness of cultures and the enduring influence of migration and exchange. It is a culinary ambassador, carrying with it the story of India's rich and diverse heritage. As you savor a samosa, wherever you may be, remember that it embodies the essence of India –

adaptable, inventive, tolerant, and heterogeneous. It is a symbol of cultural fusion, a testament to the power of food to connect people across time and space.

The samosa's narrative stretches into a deeper examination of the very concept of identity and belonging. In a world increasingly defined by globalization, the samosa challenges us to reconsider the notion of fixed cultural boundaries. Its journey, spanning millennia and continents, underscores the dynamic and fluid nature of cultural exchange. The samosa is a living testament to the fact that cultures are not static entities, but rather, constantly evolving and interacting with one another.

The samosa's story also highlights the importance of culinary traditions as a form of cultural memory. Food, in its many forms, serves as a powerful conduit for transmitting cultural values, beliefs, and practices across generations. The samosa, with its rich history and diverse variations, is a tangible link to the past, a culinary heirloom that connects us to our ancestors and their experiences.

Furthermore, the samosa's journey illuminates the role of trade and migration in shaping culinary landscapes. The ancient trade routes that connected Persia to India facilitated the exchange of goods, ideas, and culinary techniques, leading to the diffusion of the samosa and its subsequent adaptation in different regions. The migration of peoples, whether driven by conquest, economic opportunity, or social upheaval, has also played a crucial role in the dissemination of culinary traditions.

The samosa's story is not just about food; it is also about

the power of adaptation and innovation. In each new environment, the samosa has been transformed and reimagined, reflecting the local tastes and preferences of its adopted home. This adaptability is a key to its enduring popularity, allowing it to remain relevant and appealing across diverse cultures and generations.

The samosa's journey also highlights the importance of inclusivity and tolerance in cultural exchange. India's embrace of the samosa, its willingness to adapt and incorporate new ingredients and techniques, is a testament to its open and welcoming approach to cultural influences. This spirit of inclusivity is a hallmark of Indian culture, contributing to its rich and diverse culinary heritage.

In conclusion, the samosa is much more than a humble street snack. It is a culinary masterpiece, a historical artifact, and a symbol of cultural exchange. Its journey, spanning millennia and continents, is a testament to the power of food to connect people across time and space. As you savor a samosa, remember that you are partaking in a global culinary odyssey, a journey that embodies the essence of India – adaptable, inventive, tolerant, and heterogeneous. The samosa is a reminder that our identities are not defined by rigid boundaries, but rather, by the rich tapestry of experiences and influences that shape our lives.

CHAPTER SIXTEEN

BONUS FEATURE - THE FIERY FUSION: UNRAVELING THE SAGA OF INDO-CHINESE CUISINE

The tantalizing aroma of sizzling garlic, the sharp tang of soy sauce, and the fiery kick of green chilies—these are the hallmarks of Indo-Chinese cuisine, a culinary phenomenon that has captivated India for over a century. While the concept of fusion food might conjure images of contemporary chefs experimenting with exotic ingredients and avant-garde techniques, the truth is that Indo-Chinese cuisine is a testament to the enduring power of cultural exchange, a vibrant tapestry woven from the threads of two distinct culinary traditions.

Far from being a fleeting trend, Indo-Chinese food, often simply referred to as "Chinese food" or "Chindian" cuisine, has become an integral part of India's culinary landscape. It represents a fascinating fusion, a harmonious marriage of Chinese culinary techniques and seasonings with the bold, spicy flavors that define Indian gastronomy. At its core, it is an Indian interpretation of Chinese cuisine, a delicious hybrid that seamlessly blends the deep-fried, spicy flavors beloved by Indians with the distinct umami notes of soy sauce and vinegar.

The unique flavor profile of Indo-Chinese cuisine is further enhanced by the use of ingredients like Schezwan (a phonetic adaptation of Sichuan) sauce, which replaces the numbing Sichuan peppercorns with fiery dried red chilies. Manchurian-style cooking, another hallmark of this cuisine, involves battering and frying meat or vegetables, then tossing them in a spicy soy-based sauce infused with classic Indian ingredients like garlic, ginger, and green chilies.

While Indo-Chinese food has spread its culinary wings across India, its roots lie firmly planted in the vibrant city of Kolkata, formerly known as Calcutta. It is here, in the heart of India's cultural capital, that the seeds of this culinary fusion were sown, nurtured by the city's thriving Chinese community. So deeply ingrained has this cuisine become in Indian culture that many Indians genuinely believe it to be authentic Chinese food, a testament to its seamless integration into the nation's culinary identity.

The story of Indo-Chinese cuisine is inextricably linked to the history of the Chinese community in Kolkata, particularly those of Hakka origin. The Hakka people, known for their resilience and adaptability, played a pivotal role in shaping the flavors and techniques that define this unique culinary tradition.

The first Chinese settlements in Kolkata date back to 1778, but it was not until the early 20th century that a vibrant Chinatown emerged, transforming the city's culinary landscape. This bustling enclave became a melting pot of cultures, where Chinese immigrants adapted their traditional cooking to suit the local palate, giving birth to the distinctive flavors of Indo-Chinese cuisine.

Today, Indo-Chinese restaurants can be found in even the most remote corners of India, a testament to the cuisine's widespread popularity. With the advent of smartphones and online search engines, finding the perfect Indo-Chinese meal has become easier than ever. A simple search for "Indo Chinese restaurant near me" or "Indian Chinese food near me" yields a plethora of options, from street-side stalls serving up quick bites to upscale restaurants offering elaborate menus.

The foundation of Indo-Chinese cuisine lies in the clever adaptation of Chinese cooking techniques to Indian tastes. While traditional Chinese cuisine utilizes a wide range of spices and seasonings, Indo-Chinese cooking often incorporates ingredients more commonly found in Indian kitchens. Spices like cumin, coriander seeds, and turmeric, though present to some extent in the Xinjiang region of China, are used more liberally in Indian cooking, adding depth and complexity to Indo-Chinese dishes. Other key ingredients include hot chilies, ginger, garlic, sesame seeds, dried red chilies, black peppercorns, and yogurt, creating a symphony of flavors that tantalize the taste buds.

Indo-Chinese cuisine boasts a diverse array of dishes, but two stand out as particularly iconic: Schezwan and Manchurian.

Schezwan, though phonetically similar to Sichuan, represents a distinct culinary identity. While Sichuan cuisine is known for its numbing peppercorns, Schezwan dishes in India focus on a fiery blend of red chilies and garlic, creating a bold, spicy flavor that has become synonymous with Indo-Chinese food.

Manchurian, another beloved Indo-Chinese dish, typically features meat or paneer (Indian cottage cheese) and a medley of vegetables cooked in a thick, creamy, and spicy brown sauce. Legend has it that Manchurian was created by a chef named Nelson Wang, who sought to combine the simplicity of Indian ingredients like ginger, garlic, and green chilies with the umami richness of soy sauce.

The story of Indo-Chinese food is a testament to the power of culinary adaptation and innovation. It is a story of immigrants who brought their culinary traditions to a new land and, through a process of creative adaptation, gave birth to a cuisine that is both familiar and unique. It is a story of cultural exchange, where two distinct culinary traditions have come together to create something truly special.

The popularity of Indo-Chinese cuisine in India speaks to

its ability to satisfy the diverse palates of the nation. Its bold, spicy flavors, combined with the comforting familiarity of Indian ingredients, have made it a favorite among people of all ages and backgrounds. From street-side stalls to upscale restaurants, Indo-Chinese food has become an integral part of India's culinary identity.

The fusion of Chinese and Indian culinary traditions extends beyond the mere combination of ingredients and techniques. It also reflects a broader cultural exchange, a dialogue between two ancient civilizations. The Chinese community in Kolkata, through their culinary innovations, have not only enriched the city's gastronomic landscape but also contributed to the cultural fabric of India.

The story of Indo-Chinese cuisine is a reminder that food is more than just sustenance; it is a powerful expression of culture, identity, and history. It is a language that transcends borders, connecting people across continents and generations.

The spread of Indo-Chinese cuisine across India is also a reflection of the nation's evolving culinary landscape. As India has become more cosmopolitan and interconnected, its people have embraced new flavors and culinary experiences. Indo-Chinese food, with its unique blend of familiar and exotic flavors, has become a symbol of this culinary openness.

The enduring popularity of Indo-Chinese cuisine is also a testament to its versatility. Its ability to adapt to different tastes and preferences has allowed it to thrive in a diverse culinary environment. From vegetarian Manchurian to chicken Schezwan, there is an Indo-Chinese dish to satisfy every palate.

The story of Indo-Chinese cuisine is not just about the past; it is also about the present and the future. As India continues to evolve, so too will its culinary traditions. Indo-Chinese food, with its rich history and adaptable nature, is poised to remain a beloved part of India's culinary landscape for generations to come.
To truly understand the essence of Indo-Chinese cuisine, one must delve into the specific dishes that have captured the hearts and palates of Indians across the nation.

Manchurian: This iconic dish, available in both vegetarian and non-vegetarian versions, features deep-fried vegetable or meat balls coated in a thick, spicy brown sauce. The sauce, typically made with soy sauce, ginger, garlic, and green chilies, offers a harmonious blend of sweet, savory, and spicy flavors. The texture of the crispy balls contrasts beautifully with the smooth, velvety sauce, creating a delightful culinary experience.

Schezwan Noodles: These fiery noodles, often stir-fried with vegetables or meat, are a testament to the bold flavors of Indo-Chinese cuisine. The Schezwan sauce, with its intense heat from dried red chilies and garlic, coats the noodles, creating a tantalizingly spicy and aromatic dish. The addition of vegetables like bell peppers, cabbage, and carrots adds a touch of freshness and balance to the dish.

Chilli Chicken/Paneer: This dish features bite-sized pieces of chicken or paneer, battered and deep-fried, then tossed in a spicy and tangy sauce. The sauce, typically made with soy sauce, vinegar, and green chilies, offers a delightful contrast of flavors. The crispy texture of the chicken or paneer, combined with the flavorful sauce, makes this dish a popular choice among Indo-Chinese food lovers.

Vegetable Fried Rice: This classic Indo-Chinese dish features rice stir-fried with a medley of vegetables, soy sauce, and other seasonings. The addition of ingredients like shredded cabbage, carrots, and spring onions adds a touch of freshness and vibrancy to the dish. Vegetable fried rice is a versatile dish that can be enjoyed on its own or as a side dish to other Indo-Chinese delicacies.

Spring Rolls: These crispy, deep-fried rolls, filled with a mixture of vegetables or meat, are a popular appetizer in Indo-Chinese cuisine. The thin, crispy pastry encases a flavorful filling, creating a delightful contrast of textures. Spring rolls are often served with a sweet and sour dipping sauce, adding a touch of tanginess to the dish.

These are just a few examples of the many delicious dishes that make up the rich tapestry of Indo-Chinese cuisine. Each dish tells a story, a story of cultural exchange, culinary innovation, and the enduring power of food to connect people.

The story of Indo-Chinese food is a testament to the power of cultural fusion. It is a story of how two distinct culinary traditions can come together to create something truly unique and delicious. It is a story that continues to unfold, as Indo-Chinese cuisine continues to evolve and adapt to the changing tastes of India.

CHAPTER SEVENTEEN

BONUS FEATURE: THE TANGY TALE OF PANI PURI

The mere mention of Pani Puri, also known as Golgappa, evokes a sensory symphony: the crisp shatter of the puri, the explosion of tangy water, the soft bite of spiced potato. It's a street food phenomenon, a beloved indulgence that transcends social strata and geographical boundaries within India. But beyond its undeniable deliciousness lies a captivating narrative, a tale that intertwines history, mythology, and culinary ingenuity. Who, indeed, invented this iconic snack? And what is the connection between Pani Puri and the epic Mahabharata?

For those unfamiliar with this culinary gem, Pani Puri consists of a small, hollow, deep-fried sphere of semolina or wheat flour, known as a puri. This puri is then punctured, filled with a mixture of spiced mashed potatoes, chickpeas, or other fillings, and drenched in a tangy, flavored water, often made with tamarind, mint, or coriander. This water, known as "pani," is the soul of the dish, providing the essential burst of flavor that balances the savory filling.

The origins of Pani Puri are shrouded in a delightful blend of historical fact and folkloric speculation. While its exact inventor remains elusive, the earliest precursor to Pani Puri is believed to be "Phulki," a similar fried snack originating in Magadh, one of the 16 Mahajanapadas of ancient India. However, the lack of definitive historical records leaves the true architect of this culinary masterpiece shrouded in mystery.
Some historians suggest that Pani Puri emerged in the regions of Uttar Pradesh and Bihar roughly 100-125 years ago. This theory posits that Pani Puri evolved from Raj-Kachori, a larger, more elaborate snack. The idea is that someone, perhaps by chance, created a smaller version of the puri and filled it with various ingredients, leading to the birth of Pani Puri.

However, the most captivating narrative surrounding the origins of Pani Puri comes from the realm of mythology, specifically the epic Mahabharata. This legend attributes the creation of Pani Puri to none other than Draupadi, the wife of the five Pandava brothers.

The story goes that during their exile, Kunti, the mother of the Pandavas, sought to test Draupadi's resourcefulness and ability to manage scarce resources. She presented Draupadi with a small amount of leftover potato curry (sabzi) and just enough wheat dough to make a single small chapati, instructing her to ensure that the Pandavas were adequately fed.

Faced with this daunting challenge, Draupadi, known for her intelligence and ingenuity, devised a clever solution. She used the limited dough to create small, hollow puris, which she then filled with the potato curry. The result was a light, flavorful, and filling snack that satisfied the Pandavas' hunger.

Kunti, impressed by Draupadi's creativity and her ability to provide for her husbands equally, blessed the dish with immortality. This blessing, according to legend, ensured that Pani Puri would travel far and wide, evolving into various forms and names, yet remaining a beloved culinary delight.

The story of Draupadi's Pani Puri is not just a charming myth; it also offers a valuable lesson in resourcefulness and problem-solving. It demonstrates the ability to transform limited resources into something substantial and satisfying, a skill that is highly valued in both culinary and everyday life.

The legend also highlights the importance of impartiality and fairness, as Kunti's test was designed to ensure that Draupadi would treat all five Pandava brothers equally. Draupadi's successful creation of Pani Puri not only satisfied their hunger but also demonstrated her ability to manage resources fairly and efficiently.

The evolution of Pani Puri from its humble origins in Magadh or its mythological creation by Draupadi is a testament to the dynamic nature of culinary traditions. Over time, the dish has undergone numerous transformations, adapting to regional tastes and preferences.

Today, Pani Puri is known by various names across India. In Maharashtra, it is called Pani Puri, while in other regions, it is known as Golgappa, Puchka, or Gupchup. Each name reflects the regional variations in ingredients, preparation, and serving style.

In some regions, the filling consists of mashed potatoes and chickpeas, while in others, it may include sprouted lentils or other vegetables. The "pani" also varies, with some versions being tangy and spicy, while others are sweet and sour.

The serving style of Pani Puri also differs across regions. In some areas, the vendor prepares each puri individually, filling it with the desired ingredients and handing it to the customer. In other regions, the puris are pre-filled, and the customer dips them into the "pani" themselves.

Despite these variations, the essence of Pani Puri remains the same: a light, crispy puri filled with a flavorful mixture and drenched in tangy water. It is a dish that embodies the spirit of Indian street food – simple, flavorful, and satisfying.

The popularity of Pani Puri can be attributed to several factors. First, it is a highly customizable dish, allowing individuals to tailor the filling and "pani" to their specific tastes. Second, it is a light and refreshing snack, perfect for hot weather. Third, it is an affordable and accessible street food, available at countless stalls and carts across India.

Beyond its culinary appeal, Pani Puri also holds cultural

significance. It is a symbol of Indian street food culture, representing the vibrant and diverse culinary traditions of the nation. It is a dish that brings people together, fostering a sense of community and shared experience.

The story of Pani Puri also offers valuable insights into the principles of management and resource optimization. As the author of the initial text mentioned, Pani Puri demonstrates the ability to make the best use of scarce resources. Just as Draupadi transformed limited ingredients into a satisfying meal, restaurants can utilize leftover ingredients to create new and innovative Pani Puri variations, minimizing waste and maximizing profitability.

The "less is more" philosophy embodied by Pani Puri also highlights the importance of simplicity in problem-solving. Often, the most effective solutions are the simplest ones. Draupadi's ingenious approach to Kunti's challenge demonstrates the power of creative thinking and resourcefulness in overcoming obstacles.

The story of Pani Puri is a reminder that food is not just about sustenance; it is also about creativity, innovation, and cultural expression. It is a language that transcends borders, connecting people through shared experiences and culinary traditions.

The widespread popularity of Pani Puri also highlights the importance of adaptability and innovation in the culinary world. Just as the dish has evolved over time, adapting to regional tastes and preferences, restaurants and food vendors must also be willing to adapt and innovate to meet the changing needs of their customers.

The story of Pani Puri is a testament to the enduring power of culinary traditions. It is a story that has been passed down through generations, evolving and adapting along the way. It is a story that continues to resonate with people across India, reminding them of the rich and diverse culinary heritage of their nation.

The Pani Puri experience is also a testament to the sensory journey that food can provide. The contrasting textures of the crisp puri and the soft filling, combined with the explosion of flavors from the tangy "pani," create a truly unforgettable culinary experience.

The act of eating Pani Puri is also a social experience, often shared with friends and family. It is a moment of joy and laughter, a shared indulgence that strengthens bonds and creates lasting memories.

The story of Pani Puri is a reminder that food is more than just fuel for the body; it is also fuel for the soul. It is a source of comfort, joy, and connection, a way to celebrate life and culture.

In conclusion, the story of Pani Puri is a captivating blend of history, mythology, and culinary ingenuity. It is a tale that highlights the importance of resourcefulness, creativity, and adaptability. It is a story that celebrates the rich and diverse culinary traditions of India. And most importantly, it is a story that reminds us of the power of food to connect people, create memories, and bring joy to our lives.

Credits

1. The Dharma Dispatch

2. Mr. Sandeep Balakrishna

3. Keerthika Govindhaswamy

4. The Hindu Newspaper

***

THE END

(Maybe??)

www.ingramcontent.com/pod-product-compliance
Lightning Source LLC
Chambersburg PA
CBHW062216150726

47991CB00006B/2306